MARKETS, MISCONDUCT AND THE TECHNOLOGICAL AGE

MARKETS, MISCONDUCT AND THE TECHNOLOGICAL AGE

EDITED BY
DAVID CHAIKIN & DERWENT COSHOTT

AUSTRALIAN SCHOLARLY

Contents

Preface

The digital age has brought disruption to the many markets in which we operate. At the same time there has been massive violations of conduct rules by financial institutions, which have been exposed since the Global Financial Crisis in 2008. It has been estimated that more than £279 billion has been paid by financial institutions in the United States, Europe and elsewhere, including Australia, by way of fines, penalties or as compensation for breaches of conduct rules largely in the financial services markets. The issue of market misconduct and how to tackle it has been the focus of governments, regulatory agencies and inquiries; such as the Australian Royal Commission Inquiry into Misconduct in Banking, Superannuation and Financial Services.

The issue of market behaviour and the role of technology were were the subject of intensive discussion at the Annual Conference of the Discipline of Business Law at the University of Sydney Business School in November 2017. The Conference gave rise to a series of questions. Do technological advances aid or impede market misconduct? Are regulatory tools aimed at minimising market misconduct effective? Are corporate crimes such as insider trading and money laundering moving beyond the scope of detection and enforcement? How do we respond to the use of blockchain technology? What is the future for markets in the technology age? Some of these issues are explored in this book – *Markets, Misconduct and the Technological Age*. The book is a result of a collaboration of legal academics (including one of the EU's leading criminologists), practitioners and regulators.

There has been a tendency in the popular and social media to demonise financial markets, financial products and instruments by reporting only negative stories about those markets. Yet the legitimate uses of markets, whether they be onshore or offshore, are a foundation stone of modern capitalism. The English law concept of a trust has been subject to ill-informed criticism, particularly in civil law countries, which traditionally do not understand or recognise trust structures. In chapter 1, Derwent Coshott provides a detailed critique of the market for trusts, focusing on their widespread legitimate uses and users. He explains the nature of the express trust on a doctrinal and historical level; and argues that attempts to denigrate the way trusts are frequently used internationally misunderstands the trust's fundamental role in the development of Western economies. In chapter 2, David Chaikin examines the offshore secrecy market, arguing that corporate secrecy rather than bank secrecy is the major problem now faced by law enforcement. Chaikin suggests that the new whistleblowing phenomena, aka the Panama Papers, has been made possible by the digital transformation of business, resulting in a significant threat to the offshore secrecy model. In chapter 3, Rod Henderson explores the world of legal tech startups by explaining the history, theory and evolution of legal services, and then tackling two regulatory challenges – the provision of legal services by an unqualified legal practitioner, and the boundary between legal advice and legal information. Henderson suggests that regulatory reform should focus on the impact of technology on the delivery of legal services 'to benefit and meet the needs of clients/customers.'

One of the greatest threats to financial markets is insider trading which, if left unchecked, will undermine confidence of investors and thereby reduce the efficiency, if not the viability, of markets. In chapter 4, Juliette Overland examines how advances in technology have impacted both those who engage in insider trading and the regulators who are mandated to detect, investigate and prosecute insider trading. Overland suggests that the massive volume of information made possible by technology poses challenges to Australian regulators, who are required to prove in an insider trading case that the information is not 'generally available' and that it is 'material'. Overland also critiques other challenges, including: the risk of hacking of inside information from corporations, the rise of high-frequency trading which not only makes it more difficult to monitor trades, but also has the potential to reduce confidence of ordinary investors who do not have access to such technology. On the other hand, given that insiders will use technology to communicate their illegal plans, there are new opportunities for regulators to follow paper trails to detect and investigate insider trading. Overland's chapter is complemented by chapter 5, which provides an edited version of a panel discussion concerning the interrelationship between the regulatory topics of insider trading, continuous disclosure of information, and securities trading policies of listed public companies. The panel discussion was led by Overland, with the participation of two company secretaries (Rachel Launders from Nine Entertainment Co. Holdings Ltd, and Dominic Millgate from Boral Ltd) and an experienced legal practitioner (Matt Egerton-Warburton from King & Wood Mallesons). The panel discussion provided a range of practical insights into how business executives implement strategies to ensure that their companies and employees comply with the regulatory requirements, and how technology is impacting executives and their legal advisors, both internal and external.

The final two chapters provide a criminological and theoretical perspective on financial crime, and a global regulatory critique of the risks posed by new technologies. In chapter 6, Michael Levi argues that 'corporate culpability is a legal and social construction' which is heavily influenced by the political and business elites' rationalisations of ostensibly criminal conduct. Levi states that there are serious theoretical and practical questions concerning the meaning of 'legitimacy,' the relative importance of criminal law versus regulation as an enforcement strategy, as well as the nature of society labeling and sanctions in combating financial misconduct. In chapter 7, Gordon Hook, the Executive Secretary of the Asia-Pacific Group on Money Laundering, focuses on peer review evaluations of jurisdictions' implementation of the global standards on money laundering, pointing out that technology is creating new products, services and delivery channels which require financial institutions to manage and mitigate identifiable financial crime risks. Hook shows that the cost of regulatory failure is high, with the Commonwealth Bank paying a record $700 million penalty for a series of violations, including failing to carry out risk assessments of its Intelligent Deposit Machines before they were launched. Hook concludes that regulators and financial institutions that do not give proper attention to the most serious money laundering and terrorist financing risks will inevitably give criminals opportunities to exploit 'gaping holes' in their national systems.

David Chaikin and Derwent Coshott
University of Sydney

Chapter 1

The Market for Trusts: An International Overview of Their Legitimate Uses and Users

Derwent Coshott

Maitland once described the trust as the single greatest invention of English law: it 'perhaps forms the most distinctive achievement of English lawyers.'[1] Yet in recent years, the trust has become something of a dirty word. The association of the trust structure with the asset protection and tax minimisation strategies of the so-called 'super rich' has brought increasing attention on just what the trust is used for, and who uses it.[2] But this ignores the fact, as Maitland went onto argue, that the trust has been one of the longest enduring and most popularly utilised legal structures throughout the common law world, and with good cause.[3] The ability to separate the ownership and management of assets (property, money, etc.) has long been recognised as socially beneficial for all manner of reasons, such as, among others: the efficient allocation of capital; managing assets on behalf of those who are unable to; and, enabling money and property to be given freely to charitable endeavours, while ensuring donors can be safe in the knowledge that their contributions will not be misapplied or misappropriated.[4] This chapter will discuss these

---

1   Frederic W. Maitland, *Equity: A Course of Lectures* (John Brunyate ed., Cambridge University Press, 2nd revised edn., 1936) 23.

2   Spencer Woodman, 'Inside the Secret World of Offshore Mega-Trusts', *International Consortium of Investigative Journalists* (online), 7 November 2017, <https://www.icij.org/investigations/paradise-papers/secret-world-offshore-mega-trusts/>; *Schmidt v Rosewood* [2003]. 2 AC 709, 715.

3   Maitland, above n 1, 23: 'It seems to us almost essential to civilisation'.

4   See, Jonathan Garton, *Public Benefit in Charity Law* (Oxford University Press, 2013) [2.16], [3.18], [3.20]–[3.21].

and other legitimate uses of the trust, and outline why the trust should not be regarded as some kind of inherently illicit structure, used only by those who would seek to do wrong. Instead, this chapter explains what the trust actually is, and the ways it is used by people for reasons that we have long regarded as legitimate in a modern sophisticated economy. In doing so, this chapter is divided into three distinct but related parts. The first part explains what the trust actually is, and most relevantly what it is not; clearing up several misconceptions that frequently surround the trust structure. This part of the chapter correctly identifies the relational nature of the trust, and uses this to critically analyse theories of the trust that have positioned it as some kind of entity, akin to a company, or a contract-like arrangement. The second part of the chapter outlines some of the legitimate uses of trusts throughout the centuries, and the social and economic legitimacy of those uses. This part explains how the trust has always been utilised for purposes that some today regard as both legitimate (i.e. supporting charity, or managing assets on behalf of others) and somewhat illegitimate (i.e. asset protection and tax minimisation/avoidance). Yet the fact that the trust has been used for these various purposes from its earliest years, on a societal scale, indicates that many of these purposes should not be regarded as somehow wrong, and nor should the trust itself be dammed in the process. The third part of the chapter finally outlines two unique trust structures that we find in the international world of trusts today: the Non-Charitable Purpose (NCP) trust and the Spendthrift trust. This part outlines how these structures work and that, despite their seeming uniqueness, actually fit into both the understanding of the trust developed in part one, and the way trusts have been used throughout history in part two. As a result, this chapter will clarify some of the misconceptions that surround the trust, and will properly identify it as a legitimate and, ultimately, socially useful legal structure.

I. What Is the Trust?

At its simplest, the trust is a legal relationship. This relationship can exist between the trustees and the beneficiaries in a private trust; or between the trustees and the public in a charitable trust.[5] Accordingly, a trust requires beneficiaries or a valid charitable purpose.[6] If there are beneficiaries, then they must be defined with certainty: either specifically or as part of an ascertained class.[7] If however, we are dealing with a charitable trust, the charitable purpose must be one recognised by the law as valid.[8] Traditionally, these purposes included the relief of poverty, the advancement of religion, the advancement of education, and other purposes considered beneficial to society.[9] In more recent years though, various other purposes have been recognised under legislation in numerous jurisdictions.[10] All express trusts also require a settlor: the person who creates the trust; provides the trust property; and sets-out the trust's terms. Finally, and of course being a legal relationship between trustees and either beneficiaries or the public, trusts also require a trustee: the person who takes title to the trust property, and manages that property for the beneficiaries or charitable purpose.[11]

In terms of what the trust is, the above requirements are both basic and unarguable. However, this has not stopped many from characterising the trust as something other than a legal relationship of the kind described. Perhaps the most common misconception is the idea of the trust as being a kind of entity, a legal structure much like a corporation.[12] This view

---

5   Note this chapter does not include a discussion of resulting or constructive trusts. As a result, wherever the term 'trust' is used, this refers to an express trust unless otherwise stated.

6   *Leahy v AG for NSW* (1959) 101 CLR 611; *Re Denley's Trust Deed* [1969] 1 Ch 373.

7   *McPhail v Doulton* [1971] AC 424.

8   *Income Tax Special Purposes Commissioners v Pemsel* [1891] AC 531, 538.

9   Ibid.

10   For example, *Restatement (Third) of Trusts* (2003) §28; UTC § 405; *Charities Act 2013* (Cth) s 12(1); *Charities Act 2011* (Eng) s 3(1).

11   While a trust will never fail for wont of a trustee, nevertheless one must be appointed in order for the trust to function.

12   Robert H. Sitkoff, 'An Agency Costs Theory of Trust Law' (2003–2004) 89 *Cornell L. Rev.* 621; Henry Hansmann and Ugo Mattei, 'The Functions of Trust Law: A Comparative and Legal Analysis' (1998) 73 *N.Y.U. L. Rev.* 434.

primarily arises from the school of thought known as law and economics, which seeks to explain the law in economic terms.[13] The idea of the trust as an entity is based on the work of Ronald Coase and his concept of the firm, being an enterprise of some kind that is organised through a legal structure (usually a corporation).[14] Within such a model, the legal structure's role is to primarily serve as a kind of 'nexus of contracts' through which the enterprise may arrange its various legal liabilities with both internal and external parties in a cost effective manner.[15] While there is some truth to this view in the trust context, as the trust does provide a legal framework through which the liabilities of its various participants and third parties are organised; it would be a mistake to take this economic perspective and transpose it into legal reality. This is because, when dealing with a trust, a person is always dealing with the person who is the trustee; and there is no legal distinction between liabilities the trustee may incur when acting in that capacity versus when acting in their own personal capacity. Unfortunately, this fact is one that often seems to escape those people engaging in business and commerce, who may contract with a trustee thinking they are contracting with a legal entity similar to a corporation.[16] This mistake can have profound effects; especially in insolvencies where the rights of the beneficiaries to trust property are far stronger than the rights shareholders of a company may have in a similar situations.[17]

Another misconception of what the trust is, albeit a far subtler one, is the idea of the trust as a deal: as a form of third-party contract. This view is not altogether incorrect, especially in light of the basic outline of the trust structure given above. The idea of the trust as a contract primarily comes

---

13 See, Richard A. Posner, *Economic Analysis of Law* (Wolters Kluwer, 8th edn., 2011).

14 Ronald H. Coase, 'The Nature of the Firm' (1937) 4(16) *Economica* 386. See also, Ronald H. Coase, 'The Problem of Social Cost' (1960) 3 *J.L. & Econ.* 1.

15 Henry Hansmann, Reinier Kraakman and Richard Squire, 'Law and the Rise of the Firm' (2006) 119 *Harv. L. Rev.* 1333, 1397.

16 Nuncio D'Angelo, *Commercial Trusts* (LexisNexis Butterworths, 2014) [1.19].

17 For example, in due to operation of the clear accounts rule in the context of the trustee's rights of indemnity, creditors will take subject to the trustee making good any liability to the trust: *RWG Management Ltd v Commissioner for Corporate Affairs* [1985] VR 385, 398.

from the work of John Langbein, who advances a contractarian concept of the private trust.[18] This concept is simply that the trust is a deal between the settlor and the trustee for the benefit of a third-party: the beneficiary. As a result, the trust is just a form of third-party contract; the same as one might find in Europe, or those common law jurisdictions, such as in the US, where the enforcement of third party contracts are allowed.[19] Indeed, Langbein cites Maitland himself in arguing that one of the main reasons the trust took the form it did was because the common law was too primitive to recognise such third-party arrangements at the time of the trust's origins as the *use*.[20] However, while Langbein is, in a broad sense, correct regarding the trust/third-party contract analogy, the simplicity of it misses several key important differences when the trust is considered in greater detail. For example, no third-party contract gives rise to the kinds of property rights possessed by the beneficiaries of a trust; nor does a third-party contract effect the same division of legal and equitable rights that a trust does.[21] Further, parties to a third-party contract are not subject to the same kinds of fiduciary obligations that a trustee is.[22] Finally, and perhaps most importantly, the idea of a trust as contract ignores the key reality that when coming to ascertain the terms of a trust we are looking to the settlor's intention: even where the trust arises out of a contract we apply the same interpretative principles as we do to trusts being created by declaration, in which there is no deal to construe.[23]

---

18 John H. Langbein, 'The Contractarian Basis of the Law of Trusts' (1995) 105 *Yale L.J.* 625.

19 *Lawrence v Fox* 20 N.Y. 268 (1859); *Restatement (Second) of Contracts* (1981) § 302(1).

20 Langbein, above n 18, 634.

21 It may be possible for an appropriately drafted contract to do so, however this would ironically depend on the existence of equitable rights which themselves owe their existence to the trust and equity.

22 At most their duty could be described, in certain circumstances, as having a duty of 'utmost' good faith: see, *Trans-Pacific Insurance Co (Australia) Ltd v Grand Union Insurance Co Ltd* (1989) 18 NSWLR 675; Fred Hawke, 'Utmost Good Faith – What Does it Really Mean?' (1994) 6 *Ins LJ* 91; Alan Tay, 'The Duty of Disclosure and Materiality in Insurance Contracts – A True Descendant of the Duty of Utmost Good Faith?' (2002) 13 *Ins LJ* 183.

23 Digging deeper into the laws of trusts and contract respectively also yields many other differences, but these are beyond the scope of this chapter.

Therefore, while the trust being a form of third-party contract may make sense in many practical situations in which trusts arise, like above regarding the trust as an entity it does not reflect the legal reality of the trust structure; a reality that must always be kept in mind when discussing what the express trust is in order so that we may properly understand it, how it works, and what people are legitimately using it for.

The preceding discussion should also, by necessary implication, lead us to recognise something else about the trust: that just because something is called a trust does not mean it is. An example of this is statutory business trust, made famous by the US State of Delaware and now utilised in a number of other US States and jurisdictions.[24] In short, the statutory business trust, as described in the *Delaware Statutory Trust Act*, provides full limited liability protections for beneficiaries and trustees,[25] has perpetual existence by default,[26] and its own legal identity.[27] However, despite the name, this essentially means the statutory business trust is not a trust; rather, it is, functionally speaking, a company that has been emptied of almost any mandatory requirements. It is, in the words of Hansmann, Kraakman and Squire, 'the final step in the historical evolution of commercial entities.'[28] As a result, although it might bear the label of a trust, it is not. But this is not because it does not share features with the trust structure; rather, it is because it more closely resembles the company structure and lacks many of those essential features that characterise the trust.[29] For example, as

---

24 Gregory C. Walsh and Marnin J. Michaels, 'The state of statutory business trusts in the United States' (2013) 19(6) *Trusts and Trustees* 681, 686–7; Robert H. Sitkoff, 'The American Statutory Business Trust: A Research Agenda' in Hans Tijo (ed.), *Regulation of Wealth Management* (National University of Singapore, 2008) 17–35. Singapore also has provisions for such structures (*Business Trusts Act* (Singapore, cap 31A, 2004 rev. edn.)), and such structures are available in Hong Kong, but through what is known as a 'share stapled unit structure': Philippe Espinasse, *IPO: A Global Guide, Expanded Second Edition* (HKU Press, 2nd edn., 2014) 159 [2.17.1].

25 12 Del Code Ann § 3805.

26 Ibid § 3808(a).

27 Ibid § 3810(a)(2).

28 Hansmann, Kraakman and Squire, above n 15, 1397.

29 This is why one of the first things law students in equity courses are taught is how to distinguish a trust from other legal relationships that superficially appear

noted above, trusts do not offer the kind of limited liability protections to trustees that companies offer to their directors, nor prioritise the interests of creditors over shareholders, and for good reasons that go to the heart of the trust relationship. At the core of the trust structure is the idea that it exists for the benefit of people other than the trustee. That is why trustees are subject to the 'irreducible core' to act in good faith for the benefit of the beneficiaries, or the public in a charitable trust.[30] Relevantly, trustees are also subject to the 'clear accounts' rule, which prevents them from accessing trust property to satisfy any properly incurred liabilities that may have arisen in carrying out the trust where they have any unsatisfied liabilities to the trust due to a previous breach.[31] Both of these mandatory rules, together with others, act to ensure that trustees have both enforceable duties to the beneficiaries/public, and that the beneficiaries/public are placed in priority to the rights of trustees and third-party creditors. If such requirements were to be abrogated or excluded, then one may ask the question, is the trust really being run for the benefit of the beneficiaries? The point is that the rationale underlying the two legal structures – trusts and corporations – are quite different from one another, and this in turn informs the operation of their respective rules; i.e. the kind of limited liability that applies in the corporate setting does not make sense in the trust context. The idea behind the corporate structure being established and made widely available was to facilitate risky commercial ventures; i.e. to encourage people to invest their capital in various enterprises while not risking their other assets, and to encourage people to take on managing those enterprises while similarly keeping their assets safe from the risk of the enterprises failing. On the other hand, the trust is characterised by quite the opposite view of encouraging safer, risk averse investments, albeit ones being made in the same commercial

---

similar, but lack many of the inherent qualities of trusts: they may tick some of the boxes but not all of them.

30 *Armitage v Nurse* [1998] Ch 241, 253. Note, this standard also applies under US law: UTC § 105(b)(2) and (1), § 801, §1008. See also, Langbein, John H., 'Mandatory Rules in the Law of Trusts' (2004) 98 *Nw. U. L. Rev.* 1105, 1121–4.

31 See above n 17.

context.[32] This both explains why the property subject to a private trust belongs to the beneficiaries, with the differential consequences noted above, and is explicable as resulting from the fundamental fact at the core of the trust relationship: that someone other than the trustee is beneficially entitled – is the equitable owner – of the trust property. In other words, the rationale of the trust's conservative nature stems from the fact that the assets subject to the trust belong to someone other than the person with responsibility for their management, and this conservativeness can be justified in the modern social context because those assets beneficially belong to someone other than the trustee. As a result, where the trust's mandatory law is so altered as to reorient the burden and reallocate this risk, we cannot call the ensuing legal structure a trust; it is rather a trust in name only.

II. The Legitimate Uses and Users of Trusts

The preceding discussion having correctly identified what the trust is, and what it is not, enables us to now properly address the legitimate uses of trusts. To a certain extent, the trust has always been used in ways that have challenged the legal order of the day. Thus, in medieval England, trusts (in the form of *uses*) emerged as a means of mitigating the harshness of the common law so that people could benefit and utilise property in ways that were regarded as socially acceptable. For example, Maitland retells the famous stories of how medieval knights marching on crusade to the Holy Land required someone to legally manage their land while they were absent; and how Franciscan friars, who could not own land due to vows of poverty, nonetheless needed somewhere to live.[33] Due to the nature of the legal system of the time, the only way to achieve these various ends was to place the common law – legal – title to the subject land in the hands of someone else. This person, or these persons, would then voluntarily undertake to hold that property for the benefit of another – either the

---

32 Note, this does not deny that trusts are also used to split the liabilities of the various participants in the trust relationship; rather, it is about trusts encouraging behaviour geared more towards safely managing beneficiaries' assets.

33 Maitland, above n 1, 25.

Christian crusader, or the Franciscan friars: an arrangement that would become known as the *use*, and later the trust. Of course, as is also well known, such arrangements were not actionable at common law, and so their enforcement lay with the Kings who retained a residual power to, as per their coronation oaths, 'do equal and right justice and discretion in mercy and truth'.[34] In other words, to act according to conscience, being the medieval concept of a mental faculty that could discern moral right and wrong.[35] As with many other aspects of governance, the Kings delegated this power to another, the Chancellor, who enforced these *uses* according to conscience, which given the early Chancellors were almost always Catholic priests, was invariably a manifestation of Christian doctrine.[36] Yet despite the fact the Chancellors acted according to Christian standards – the socially acceptable standards of right and wrong at the time – in enforcing *uses*, nevertheless the Chancellors' actions represented a subversion of the letter of the common law, if not its spirit, because they were in effect making orders that were contrary to a person's strict legal rights at common law; i.e. it may be against conscience to resile from a promise to hold property for the benefit of another, but at common law a person was free to do so.

As time went on however, people learned to utilise the *use* in more subversive ways, which the Chancellor nevertheless continued to enforce. The earliest example is the role the *use* played in avoiding the effects of the feudal incidents of landholding: primogeniture,[37] wardship and marriage,[38]

---

34 See, the Coronation Oath of King Edward II.

35 J.H. Baker, *An Introduction to English Legal History* (Oxford University Press, 4th edn., 2002) 105–8.

36 Ibid.

37 Primogeniture is the term used to represent how real property was inherited in medieval times. Unlike today, real property could not be left in a will; rather, it descended to the eldest male son, which meant younger children could only be provided for through personal property. The *use* could subvert the operation of primogeniture because primogeniture only applied to real property a person legally held at common law. If a person held real property as a *cestui que use* then primogeniture had no role to play, and its operation could be avoided by ensuring that the relevant real property was always held by living *feoffees to uses*.

38 Wardship and marriage represented a lord's rights to control the land and marriages of underage tenants whose parents had passed on. Lords could make large sums of

relief,[39] dower,[40] and forfeiture.[41] In this context, the popularity of the *use* was not so much based on the idea that equity had come to fulfil the conscience of a common law whose rigidity prevented it from acting in a broad sense, but more on the application of the broad principles that had been developed with respect to the *use* in a narrower context: i.e. people could utilise the *use* to avoid the effects of feudal incidents not because the application of those incidences was against conscience per se, but because the recognition of the *use*, and the logic of how conscience applied to an individual's voluntary undertakings, enabled people to effectively own property in equity while not owning it at common law, which is what the incidents attached to. The fact that Henry VIII's efforts to outlaw the *use*, and restore the financial benefits of feudalism to the English Crown, failed, is not a denial of the reality that people were utilising the *use* to subvert the common law; rather, it was simply the result of the fact that people had been utilising the *use* in this way for so long that it was far too late to turn back the clock, as the functional legal arrangements that resulted were, by this time, broadly regarded as socially legitimate. In other words, in this social context it was the common law that was socially wrong; and it was equity that reflected the social will of the times.

As feudalism faded from the English legal landscape, there nevertheless remained a need for the *use* structure, which evolved into the trust we know

---

money from these rights. However, wardship and marriage both depended upon a child inheriting a legal interest in the land (i.e. through primogeniture), which means the *use* could be utilised to avoid a lord's control of underage heirs.

39 Relief (and, in the case of the King's tenants-in-chief, primer seisin) represented the right of a lord to receive a payment of money when a new tenant inherited, or came into, a legal estate in real property. Again, because the *use* did not deal in such interests, because when equitable interests were inherited or transferred there was no relief to be paid.

40 Dower represented the right of a widow to a life estate in a share of her husband's real property on his passing. This right covered not only land held upon his passing, but also all land he previous held and subsequently alienated. However, dower only applies to legal interests, and so did not apply to equitable interests held under a *use*.

41 Forfeiture meant that if a person were convicted of a felony their legal interests in land would be forfeit. Again though, this only applied to legal interests; it did not apply to equitable interests held under a *use*.

today. As noted above, the *use* did not originate solely from a desire to avoid feudal incidents; it emerged from a social need for a legal structure that would enable property to be held and managed on behalf of others. This need was especially apparent in the 18th and 19th centuries, when concerns regarding taxation largely receded into history and the economies of Western nations shifted from land to personal property: from tangible to intangible wealth. But in order to build that wealth, it needed to be managed, and this came to increasingly require specialist skills: one may have material wealth but not the financial knowhow to build that wealth in a complex market place.[42] Further, the corporation was not yet available, and even when it was it was not only still in its infancy.[43] As a result, investing in commercial enterprises could be quite risky without any kind of limited liability protection for its participants: e.g. a person investing in a commercial endeavour could risk being regarded as a partner of the enterprise and so be fully legally liable for its activities. Accordingly, it was in this social context that the trust was utilised as means of both managing wealth on behalf of others who were either unwilling or unable to, and to protect the assets of investors from the risks associated with carrying out various commercial enterprises; hence the rise of the joint-stock companies and their success during this period.[44]

These examples of how people utilised the *use* and the trust are not simply matters of historical interest; they actually represent the differing roles of the trust today and sit at the core of debates surrounding what are legitimate and illegitimate uses of it. It is undoubted that the trust serves important functions in managing assets on behalf of others who are unable to, such as minors and the disabled. In the context of charities, it also provides a means of ensuring that money, or other assets, are donated to

---

42 Chantal Stebbings, *The Private Trustee in Victorian England* (Cambridge University Press, 2002) Chapter 5 'Trustees in the Commercial Context'.

43 The corporation was arguably not as well suited for the same kinds of tasks as the trust is in terms of investing wealth; although in terms of carrying out certain business activities the corporation is undoubtedly better, as demonstrated by its wide-spread use and success.

44 Hansmann, Kraakman and Squire, above n 15, 1384.

worthy causes. Indeed, testamentary trusts give people the ability to ensure that their loved ones are looked after in the event of their passing. No one would seriously argue that these uses of the trust structure are in any way illegitimate; they represent the modern manifestation of the Christian crusader and Franciscan friar examples discussed above. However, the other use of the trust – as a means of subverting legal obligations – is a different story. Is it okay, or legitimate, to use one legal structure to escape legal obligations that one would otherwise be subject to? Many have argued no, it is not,[45] but this fundamentally misunderstands certain realities about the law and its role in societies and modern commercial economies: the law has long recognised that the social and economic benefits of certain legal structures outweighs their detriments or risks of misuse. If it were otherwise then the corporation, with its limited liability protections, must come in for serious questions, especially when one considers the trust's liability protections are far weaker. Further, the law has long recognised that there are exceptions to many legal rules, and while, if looked at in a narrow way, one can make the argument that these exceptions subvert those rules, this would be to ignore the whole rationale of equity, which was to address the shortcomings and failings of the common law by supporting and, where necessary, overriding the common law: equity itself has always been an exception to the common law This is why, as Maitland's stated, 'equity had come not to destroy the common law, but to fulfil it.'[46]

III. Unique Types of Trusts

The preceding discussion has explained what the trust is and how it has been historically used: as a means of splitting the ownership and management of property, and as a means of protecting ones assets from the operation of other laws. The above has also shown how these functions

---

45 For example, Dale Boccabella, 'Family trusts often cause more harm than good' *The Conversation*, 6 April 2017, <http://theconversation.com/family-trusts-often-cause-more-harm-than-good-81551>.

46 Frederic W. Maitland, *Equity also the Forms of Action at Common Law* (A.H. Chaytor and W.J. Whittaker eds, Cambridge University Press, 1909) 17.

of the trust structure are perfectly legitimate because this is how the trust has been utilised for a number of centuries. In light of this, it is worthwhile considering a unique trust structure that, while a creature of legislative alteration to the trust structure, nevertheless meets the criteria of the trust and how it has been used discussed above: the Non-Charitable Purpose (NCP) trust.

The NCP trust represents a legislative creation prevalent in several so-called 'offshore' jurisdictions. They were enacted primarily in response to concerns regarding the use of charitable trusts in asset securitisation schemes where property was transferred to a company, which would serve as the subject of the trust. The trust would be established to advance some recognised charitable purpose such as religion, or the relief of poverty, in favour of a named charity. Meanwhile, securities would be issued by the company on its property, and the income from this property would be paid to security holders. At the conclusion of this arrangement, the company would be wound up, and any remaining funds paid to the charitable purpose. Naturally, this would consist of very little if anything being paid to the named charity, and so there were doubts over whether this arrangement would hold up to legal scrutiny.

However, there was, and remains, a legitimate commercial desire for these sorts of arrangements. Asset securitisation arrangements of this kind are frequently utilised by financial institutions throughout the world, and are subject to assessments by international ratings agencies. As a result, offshore jurisdictions, seeing the economic advantages in facilitating the creation of such arrangements, enacted the NCP trust, which did away with the charitable purpose requirements that were the cause of the concern. Therefore, NCP trusts are pure purpose trusts, in the sense they do not have legal beneficiaries and are not for recognised charitable purposes; even though people economically benefit from the trust, they are not legal beneficiaries and are not entitled to enforce the trust. This does not mean though, that NCP trusts are unenforceable like pure purpose trusts under Anglo-Australian law. NCP trusts, through legislation, provide for third-party trust enforcers to exercise the enforcement functions usually exercised by beneficiaries in private trusts and the Attorney-General in charitable trusts.[47] Further, like true charitable trusts, they can be of unlimited duration. Therefore, NCP trusts are a sort of modified charitable trust, in the sense that they are established for purposes, not people (like charitable trusts), even if those purposes are simply to hold property on trust.

Given the above, why is the NCP also not a trust in name only as with respect to the Delaware statutory business trust? The reason is because, despite its alterations to trusts law, the NCP trust structure is still one established for the benefit of people with enforceable duties on the parts of its trustees. While scholars have made the argument that trusts do not require beneficiaries, only enforcers,[48] this misses a fundamental reality: someone is going to derive some kind of benefit from a trust, otherwise why would anyone establish it? The key is whether enforcement and benefit needs to rest in the same individual in order for a trust to be valid. The logic of charitable trusts would say no, because of the fact that, in the charitable context, it never has, except on a broad level where the Attorney-General is said to enforce charitable trusts on behalf of the public as its representative. Even if this is accepted as a valid argument, which it is on a doctrinal level, then we still arrive at a point where trusts law accepts that in order for a trust to be valid, in terms of benefiting others, so long as the benefit is one that is seen as advancing a purpose deemed to be socially good, then it is perfectly acceptable the people benefiting from the purpose are not necessarily the ones with the power to enforce (absent legislative intervention giving them such power). If the facilitation of commercial conduct of the kind people utilise NCP trusts for is such a social good, in terms of delivering broad economic benefits, and one recognised as such by a competent legislature, then providing no other mandatory aspects of

---

47 Note, through legislative action, standing to enforce has also been extended to persons other than the Attorney-General in Australian jurisdictions (*Trustee Act 1925* (ACT) ss 94A–94E; *Charitable Trusts Act 1993* (NSW) ss 5–7; *Trusts Act 1973* (Qld) s 106; *Trustee Act 1936* (SA) ss 60–69; *Supreme Court Civil Procedure Act 1932* (Tas) s 57(2); *Charities Act 1978* (Vic) s 7L; *Charitable Trusts Act 1962* (WA) s 21) and in England (*Charities Act 2011* (Eng) s 115).

48 David Hayton, 'Developing the Obligation Characteristic of the Trust' (2001) 117 *LQR* 96.

trusts law are negatively affected there is no reason not to regard NCP trusts as valid, legitimate trust structures. Indeed, the fact there is a fierce international market for the business these kinds of trusts attract, with many so-called 'midshore' jurisdictions enacting legislation in supporting these kinds of arrangements,[49] combined with the reality that commercial purposes are increasingly being recognised as charitable under Anglo-Australian law, means it would be foolish to view NCP trusts is inherently illegitimate, or those who would use them as doing something wrong.[50]

IV. Conclusions

This chapter began with discussing the nature of the express trust and properly distinguished it as a unique legal structure, with its own rationale and functions that render it distinct from other legal structures, even those that happen to use the 'trust' name, such as the Delaware statutory business trust. The chapter then moved on to briefly explain how the trust developed, and the background to that development, in order to properly locate the trust in its social and economic context: one in which the avoidance of the operation of the common law was inherent to its success. The purpose of this part was to explain how the trust being utilised in such a way – as an exception to the operation of the common law – served a fundamental role in the development of English society and the economy, and therefore considering similar uses of the trust today as somehow being illegitimate is misguided. Finally, this chapter considered the offshore NCP trust, a frequent target for those who point to the illegitimate nature of trusts, and

---

49 Marcus Hinkley, *Is Hong Kong's trust law a threat to the offshore trust industry?* (14 October 2013) Hubbis, cited in David Chaikin and Eve Brown, *Global Competitiveness and Exporting Financial Services: A proposal for an Alternative Australian Trusts Act* (10 January 2017) Financial Services Council, 16 <http://fsi.gov.au/files/2014/05/FSC_appendix_AATA_report.pdf>.

50 See, *Crystal Palace Trustees v Minister of Town and Country Planning* [1951] 2 Ch 132 at 142; *Commissioner of Taxation v The Triton Foundation* (2005) 147 FCR 362; *Tasmanian Electronic Commerce Centre Pty Ltd v Commissioner of Taxation* (2005) 142 FCR 371 at 389; *Chamber of Commerce and Industry of Western Australia (Inc) v Commissioner of State Revenue* [2012] WASAT 146; *Grain Growers Limited v Chief Commissioner of State Revenue* [2015] NSWSC 925.

demonstrated how, both in light of the doctrinal and historical discussions in parts one and two of this chapter, the view that somehow there is something wrong with these kinds of trusts must be incorrect. Overall, this chapter has therefore demonstrated how, when critiquing both the formulation and use of legal structures, such as trusts, it is necessary to have an accurate understanding of both how those structures actually function, and the socio-economic context in which they operate. Adopting a myopic view of such structures will only lead one astray, and render one's criticisms as being less than useless in addressing whatever actual problems are caused by the usage of these legal structures domestically and internationally.

Chapter 2

Offshore Financial Secrecy and Crime in the Technological Age

David Chaikin

The concept of offshore financial secrecy is based on the famed Swiss bank secrecy brand which has been subject to massive changes since the UBS scandal in 2014. The demand for offshore financial secrecy has been driven by both legal and illegal motives. As long ago as 2006, Professor Ingo Walter suggested that important drivers of offshore private banking include tax avoidance/tax evasion, capital flight, business and family confidentiality, asset protection, insider trading, corruption and other illegal conduct requiring money laundering.[1] To this list may be added estate planning, particularly the avoidance of heirship laws or succession laws of many European civil law countries, and politically linked crimes such as terrorist financing, arms trafficking and sanctions busting.

There are many legitimate demands for offshore private banking (and by extension demands for offshore financial secrecy) from key target markets, including traditional 'high net worth' individuals and families, entrepreneurs, professionals, executives, entertainers and artists, sports professionals, intermediaries and external asset managers.[2] Nevertheless, whatever the philosophical justification of offshore financial secrecy,[3] it is significant that the competing concept of transparency of financial information has become one of the dominant cultural norms of the 21st

---

1   Ingo Walter, *Secret money: the shadowy world of tax evasion, capital flight and fraud*, 2006, Unwin Publishers.

2   See David Chaikin, 'Policy and Fiscal Effects of Swiss Bank Secrecy' (2005) 15 *Revenue Law Journal* 90, 93.

3   Ibid 94–5.

century.[4] This is illustrated by the pejorative and negative connotation of the idea of secrecy, which increasingly is associated with abuse of political or economic power.[5]

This chapter will first examine the components of offshore financial secrecy in Switzerland and its exceptions in the facilitation of international financial crime. It will then discuss the practical dimensions of financial secrecy laws and their enforcement through prosecution of economic espionage offences in Switzerland. It will argue that the new paradigm of large-scale whistleblowing in offshore financial centres has undermined, if not become an existential threat to, the continuation of financial secrecy. Finally, it will discuss how changes in technology have made a significant contribution to the disruption of offshore financial secrecy.

I. Offshore Financial Secrecy

From a legal perspective, offshore financial secrecy has three components. Firstly, there is bank secrecy whereby information concerning a bank customer obtained in the course of a banking relationship is subject to confidentiality requirements. For bank secrecy jurisdictions, this entails an additional element, namely that it is a criminal offence to breach bank secrecy. Secondly, there is corporate secrecy, whereby the ownership or control of 'corporate entities', including companies, partnerships and trusts, is kept secret.[6] Thirdly, there is professional secrecy, whereby certain professions, most noticeably lawyers, are subject to legal restrictions concerning disclosure of information about their clients.

With a few noticeable exceptions, offshore banking secrecy has never been absolute. For example, Swiss law has long recognised exceptions to the criminal prohibition on disclosure of bank information under article

---

4   See Andrea Bianchi and Anne Peters (eds.), *Transparency in International Law* (Cambridge University Press, 2013) 1.

5   Ibid 1–2.

6   See David Chaikin and Gordon Hook, *Corporate and Trust Structures: Legal and Illegal Dimensions* (Australian Scholarly Publishing, 2018). It should be noted that a trust is not a separate legal entity but is frequently and inaccurately described as a legal person.

47 of the Swiss Banking Law. The principal exceptions are: where a Swiss court orders a bank to make disclosure; where Swiss law allows disclosure (for example, Swiss banks are required to report suspicious transactions concerning their clients); and where a client consents to disclosure.[7] These exceptions to Swiss bank secrecy are also found in the offshore laws of the estimated 70 countries which have modelled their bank secrecy laws on Switzerland.[8]

Over time, the scope of the exceptions to Swiss bank secrecy have grown which have had the effect of expanding the scope of Swiss co-operation with foreign countries in investigating financial crimes. This is significant because of the principle of dual criminality which applies to foreign requests to obtain banking information in Switzerland; this means that if an alleged foreign offence is not a crime in Switzerland, the Swiss authorities cannot provide banking information. However, in the past 30 years, Switzerland has criminalised a variety of 'business conduct', such as money laundering, insider trading, market manipulation and foreign bribery, thereby allowing enlarged investigatory co-operation with foreign countries. The most important weakness in Switzerland's capacity to provide legal assistance in criminal matters has been the failure of Switzerland to criminalise tax evasion; this failure has meant that the Swiss system of mutual assistance in criminal matters is not available in cases of criminal tax evasion.[9]

In recent years more problematical than bank secrecy has been corporate secrecy in offshore financial centres, and particularly the role of international business companies (IBCs) in facilitating crime. IBCs are frequently criticised for their inherent secrecy, for example, permitting nominee ownership of shares, nominee directors and bearer share facilities, as well as a lack of public record of financial information. However, with

---

7   See Chaikin, above n 2, 99–100.

8   For example, see section 47 of the Banking Act of Singapore. See generally Rose-Marie Antoine, *Confidentiality in Offshore Financial Law* (Oxford University Press, 2002).

9   See David Chaikin, 'Corrupt Practices involving Offshore Financial Centres', in Adam Graycar and Russell G Smith, (eds.) *Handbook of Global Research and Practice in Corruption* (Edward Elgar, 2013) 203, 206–8.

the exception of bearer shares, most of these secrecy features are also available to private companies in common law jurisdictions, such as the United States and Australia. A more important policy gap is the failure of jurisdictions, including Switzerland, to implement the Financial Action Task Force Recommendations in relation to transparency of beneficial ownership of both companies and trusts.[10]

II. Offshore Financial Secrecy: A Practical Dimension

The effectiveness of offshore financial secrecy does not merely depend on the scope of the law but also the practices of banks and the enforcement policy of governments. The Swiss experience is illuminating.

In the 1980s and 1990s major Swiss banks and financial institutions in offshore secrecy jurisdictions spent 100s of millions of dollars in creating operational systems to protect the secrets of their valued clients. It was not just a matter of giving a client a numbered account, which ensured that only a limited number of persons in a bank knew the identity of a customer. The Swiss banks developed a private banking account network (PBAN) whereby banking information concerning a specific client could only be accessed typically by the relationship manager, the head of compliance and senior management. Those employees were required to use three levels of password security in order to access client information and were subject to 'sophisticated surveillance and auditing systems'.[11] One leading Swiss bank asserted that it was technically impossible for a foreign branch of a Swiss bank to access through computer any bank accounts at the Swiss bank's headquarters PBAN.[12] That is, there was a territorial blockage to prevent

---

10 See Gordon Hook, 'Beneficial Ownership and Control of Corporate and Trust Structures: Global AML/CTF Standards', in Chaikin and Hook, above n 6, 86–107.

11 See Chaikin, above n 2, 101–3. The information concerning Swiss private banking security is based on a series of confidential interviews that the author conducted in the period 1997–1999. See David Chaikin, *Electronic Threat and Defences – Hacking and Internet Banking*, Paper presented at the 4th International Financial Fraud Convention, London, 27 May 1999.

12 See affidavit of Dr P. Altorfer dated 29 September 1997, submitted to the US District Court Central District of California, in the case of *In Re Thelma L Argenal v*

access. In Switzerland, there were also restrictions to access banking information, for example, if a client opened up a Swiss bank account in the name of an offshore corporation at the Geneva branch of UBS, it was said to be impossible for any compliance manager at UBS in Zurich to search for the existence of that account.

Another feature of the bank secrecy system was the willingness of Swiss bankers and fiduciaries to mislead and/or lie to foreign law enforcement agencies and tax authorities so as to conceal their clients' banking activities and transactions. Let me give an example of what are commonly known as back-to-back loans.[13] A Swiss bank would lend money to an Australian company using the owner of that company's secret bank account as collateral for the loan. The beneficial owner of the company was able to access their undeclared monies, while at the same time the Australian company might be able obtain a tax deduction for interest payments on this business loan. It was common practice for Swiss banks to lie about this transaction by confirming that the loan was fully collateralised and that the source of the collateral was independent of the borrower. This was a useful mechanism to prevent disclosure of a Swiss bank account, particularly in circumstances where it contained the proceeds of crime, and was used to perpetuate crimes, such as insider trading, or was merely a secret depositary of funds which had not been disclosed to the tax authorities.

One significant challenge for Swiss banks was the risk that agents of foreign governments or foreign private groups would engage in economic espionage for the purpose of obtaining secret banking or financial information. Under article 271(1) of the Swiss Penal Code, it is a crime for a person to engage in information-gathering conduct on Swiss territory (without official authorisation) which is 'reserved to a public authority or a public official' where such conduct is carried out on behalf of a foreign

---

Union Bank of Switzerland et al, Case No CV 97-6605R(MCx), Hon M.L. Real presiding. Robert Swift, counsel for Argenal, supplied this affidavit to the author.

13 This is also known as loan-back money laundering. For a list of warning signs in relation to loan-back money laundering, see OECD, *Money Laundering Awareness Handbook for Tax Examiners and Tax Auditors,* Centre for Tax Policy and Administration, OECD, 2009, 43–6.

party or any other foreign organisation. It is also a crime under article 273 of the Swiss Penal Code to obtain any 'industrial or business secret' for the purpose of making it available to a foreign state, foreign organisation or a foreign private party. These two offences are known as economic espionage offences.[14] They are the key offences that the Swiss authorities rely on to protect financial secrets in Switzerland; they are designed to prevent foreign governments circumventing Swiss procedures for international co-operation.

The Swiss authorities' enforcement record is reflected in the statistics. A 2016 academic study found that, between 1960 and 2014, 97 convictions were recorded in Switzerland for breaches of article 273 of the Penal Code.[15] The study did not disclose the names of foreign countries which had sought Swiss business secrets through economic espionage. However, an earlier Swiss government report identified the following 13 countries as engaged in economic espionage to secure Swiss bank secrets in the period 1989 to 1999: France, India, Korea,[16] Israel, Philippines, Romania, Poland, Russia, Rwanda, South Africa, Yugoslavia, the United States and Zaire.

The above-mentioned violations of Swiss law were carried out at the instigation of foreign governments; for example, the case concerning the Philippines involved an agent of the Presidential Commission on Good Government who sought to find the secret bank accounts of the deposed President of the Philippines, Ferdinand Marcos, his family and business cronies.[17] A characteristic of these cases is that they were targeted economic

---

14　For an analysis of economic espionage offences in Switzerland, see David Chaikin, 'The Impact of Swiss Principles of Mutual Assistance on Financial and Fiscal Crimes' (2006) 16 *Revenue Law Journal* 192, 194–8.

15　See Catherine Konopatsch (2016), *Economic Espionage in Austria and Switzerland – latest developments in EU and a non-EU member state*, WISKOS, University of Bern, 22 September, 4, http://wiskos.de/files/pdf3/2._Economic_and_industrial_espionage_in_Austria_and_Switzerland.pdf.

16　The report merely stated Korea; it did not identify whether it was North Korea or South Korea. See Swiss Government (2000) *Report on the Protection of the State for the year 1999,* Swiss Federal Department of Justice and Police, Bern, 2000.

17　For details about the Marcos case, see David Chaikin and J.C. Sharman, *Corruption and Money Laundering: A Symbiotic Relationship* (Palgrave MacMillan, New York, 2009), 153–86.

espionage, that is they concerned only a limited number of politically connected foreign clients of Swiss banks and financial institutions. In many of the cases, the foreign government or foreign agent was suspected of paying internal employees or contractors of Swiss financial institutions to secure the confidential information.

III. The New Whistleblower Phenomena

The nature of violations of Swiss bank secrecy and economic espionage laws has dramatically changed in recent years. It is noteworthy that there has been a significant expansion of the number of 'whistleblowers' in the Swiss financial sector, and this is 'probably only the tip of the iceberg'.[18] Indeed, whistleblowers of financial secrets, who are not protected by Swiss laws, continue to supply confidential data about individual clients of banks to third parties. However, since about 2002, there has been a new type of whistleblowing in that there has been a series of massive confidential 'data dumps' by whistleblowers, many of whom have not been motivated by financial reward. These cases have not only involved Switzerland, but other offshore jurisdictions.

Some of the reported cases have identified the whistleblower, such as the case of Liechtenstein Global Trust/Liechtenstein (Heinrich Kieber), HSBC Private Bank Suisse SA/Switzerland (Herve Faliciani), Julius Baer/Cayman Islands (Rudolf Elmer) and Pricewaterhouse Coopers/Luxembourg (Antoine Deltour). While the identities of the 'whistleblowers' in the above cases are known, the identities of the individuals behind some of the biggest offshore whistleblower disclosures (such as the Panama Papers, Offshore Leaks, Bahamas Papers and Paradise Papers) have not been discovered. A brief analysis of two of these whistleblower disclosures is found below.

---

18 Saverio Lembo and Christopher Hensler (2015), *Whistleblowers in the Swiss Banking Sector: Legal Hurdles to Cooperating with Foreign Governments*, January 2015, Baer and Karrer SA <http://www.baerkarrer.ch/publications/BK%20Briefing_Whistleblowers%20in%20the%20CH%20Banking%20Sector.pdf>.

A. Panama Papers

The 2016 Panama Papers is a new 'whistleblowing phenomena' in both the nature and scale of the 'data dump'. It consists of approximately 2.6 terabytes of data,[19] about 11.5 million documents concerning the records of 214,000 offshore companies, foundations and trusts which Mossack Fonesca (Mossfon), a Panama corporate services provider/law firm, had established on behalf of its clients. That so much original source documentation was able to be 'stolen' from one firm, with the perpetuator able to avoid detection, is an extraordinary testimony to the weakness of financial privacy safeguards in the modern internet eco-system. Indeed, the fact that Mossfon's entire data base of client records over a 40-year period was 'stolen' indicates an unprecedented level of lax computer security systems. For example, several computer security experts have alleged that Mossfon's 'front-end computer systems ... [were] outdated and riddled with security flaws', and that there was no effective firewall, making the firm an easy target for a hacker.[20] However, it is not clear whether Mossfon was externally hacked, or whether a malicious insider(s) at the firm was responsible for the massive leak/theft.[21] In any event, the significance of a computer breach for the firm's reputation and the legal risk of the firm to its clients was immense, resulting in the liquidation of Mossfon and the arrest and prosecution of its founders. The impact of the Panama Papers has been dramatic, leading to the removal of the Prime Minister of Pakistan, as well as the prosecution and/or resignation of numerous politicians and business

---

19 One terabyte of data is equal to the data contained in approximately one million books.

20 See Matt Burgess and James Temperton, 'The security flaws at the heart of the Panama Papers', *Wired*, 6 April 2016, <http://www.wired.co.uk/article/panama-papers-mossack-fonseca-website-security-problems>.

21 See Danny Palmer, 'Malicious insiders the fastest growing threat to cyber security, warns report', 20 January 2016, *Computing*, citing Ernst and *Young's 2016 Global Forensic Data Analytics Survey, Shifting into high gear: mitigating risks and demonstrating returns,* <http://www.ey.com/gl/en/services/assurance/fraud-investigation---dispute-services/ey-shifting-into-high-gear-mitigating-risks-and-demonstrating-returns>.

leaders.[22] There is extensive evidence that the revelations of the Panama Papers have proved to be very useful for tax authorities in countries such as Australia and for law enforcement in developing countries.[23]

B. Paradise Papers

In 2018 there was an even more sensational leakage/theft of data from one of the world's leading offshore law firms, Appleby, two corporate service providers (Estera and Asiaciti Trust) and the corporate registries of 19 small offshore financial centres. The Paradise Papers has been presented as the largest leak/theft of confidential financial documents in modern financial history. The Paradise Papers consist of 13.4 million documents totalling about 1.4 terabytes of information relating to 120,000 individuals and corporate entities. The Paradise Papers 'data set' covered the period 1950 to 2016. In contrast to the Panama Papers, where Mossfon did not publicly explain the circumstances surrounding its loss, Appleby has asserted that the theft was the result of a sophisticated hacking operation which has injured the financial privacy of its innocent clients. Subsequently, Appleby sued a number of media outlets, including the Guardian newspaper in the United Kingdom and other media partners of the International Consortium of Investigative Journalists; the legal suit was based on a claim of breach of confidence which was settled in 2018 on undisclosed terms.[24] It seems that the majority of documents was not subject to legal professional privilege[25] but concerned Appleby's fiduciary/corporate service business which it

22 For a comprehensive account of the impact of the Panama Papers, see the website of the International Consortium of Investigative Journalists, <https://www.icij.org/>.

23 See David Chaikin, 'Law Enforcement Implications of the Panama Papers', in Chaikin and Hook, above n 6, 108–21.

24 See Appleby settles Paradise Papers litigation against Guardian and BBC, *Guardian*, 5 May 2018.

25 See the High Court decision in *Glencore International AG v Commissioner of Taxation* [2019] HCA 26 which held that, even if the Appleby documents were protected by legal professional privilege, the privilege did not apply where Glencore was seeking an injunction against the Commissioner from using or relying on the privileged advice in carrying out the Commissioner's functions. The High Court held that legal professional privilege was merely a 'shield' and could not be relied on as a 'sword'.

sold in 2016.[26] Further, despite claims that the Paradise Papers disclosed massive offshore tax crimes, the evidence so far seems to suggest that much of the information concerned tax avoidance and/or tax planning of high net worth individuals and over 100 multinational corporations.

C. The Technological Dimension

Until relatively recently, it was nearly impossible to steal bank and corporate secrets on a massive scale. What then has changed which has resulted in such gross breaches of offshore financial secrecy laws? The global digitisation of financial data, the delivery of financial services through the Internet, as well as the massive rise of international banking and the professionalism of cyber-attacks, are the obvious explanations for the increased vulnerabilities of bank security systems. In 2018 the Chief Executive of the Swiss Financial Market Supervisory Authority (FINMA) in Switzerland observed that cyber-attacks are the most important operational risk facing financial institutions in Switzerland. According to Mark Branson of FINMA, the opportunity for hacking of computer systems has grown with the rise of global digitisation of financial data.[27]

The unintended consequences of the digital transformation in private banking is summarised in a 2015 expert report:[28]

> As customer interactions increasingly take place over digital channels, banks need to take extra measures to protect customer, employee and other business data against theft, loss and cyberattacks. Multi-layered security, strict data security standards, advanced analytics and threat intelligence systems can ensure data privacy and security.

26 See Fergus Shiel, 'Paradise Papers: ICIJ partners and Appleby agree to settlement', *ICIJ*, 4 May 2018, <https://www.icij.org/blog/2018/05/paradise-papers-icij-partners-appleby-agree-settlement/>.

27 Michael Shield, 'Cyber-attacks biggest risk for Swiss banks', *Reuters*, 27 March 2018.

28 See Cognizant, *Digital Transformation in European Private Banking*, April 2015, <https://www.cognizant.com/InsightsWhitepapers/digital-transformation-in-european-private-banking-codex1296.pdf>.

Banks should continuously upgrade their security systems and prepare contingency plans while educating clients about potential fraud and cybersecurity. Private banks can take a cue from the airline industry, which has balanced its need for high security with advancements in the digital customer experience, resulting in enhanced customer security.

Financial institutions have also become vulnerable to data breaches, as they have outsourced various functions to third parties, such as service providers.[29] Here, the risk of hacking arises from third party vendors and partners which have weak computer security systems. To deal with this risk, financial institutions will typically have strict data protection clauses in their contracts, but these do not appear to provide sufficient assurance unless there is regular auditing and enforcement of such contract terms. The risk of data leakage/theft is even greater when computer security systems are outsourced to third party experts. As bank regulators have noted, it is vital that management pay close attention to the cyber capabilities, security and control systems of third parties, or otherwise they will be vulnerable to data leakage/theft.

Another factor is that banks have not been willing to pay for IT security at any cost, particularly because European private banks (especially Swiss banks) have lost their capacity to 'charge a premium for bank secrecy services'.[30] This has arisen because of the declining profitability of private banking and the dramatic increase in regulatory fines on misbehaving banks, estimated to amount to more than $273 billion since the Global Financial Crisis.[31] The effect has been that private banks in Switzerland are under great pressure to reduce costs, which may result in compromised or weak security.[32] This view is supported by surveys carried out by

---

29 See Rajiv Gupta, 'The Panama Papers Signal a New Kind of Cyber Attack', *Fortune*, 9 April 2016, http://fortune.com/2016/04/09/panama-papers-mossack-fonseca.

30 See Cognizant, above n 28.

31 Eshe Nelson, 'The bill for banks behaving badly since the financial crisis: $273 billion and counting', *Quartz*, 19 July 2017, citing a Moody's report.

32 This statement is based on a confidential interview with a former employee of a

MyPrivateBanking research which found that the 'majority of private bankers and wealth managers worldwide showed little regard for the protection of personal data on public websites'.[33] In particular, it found that 61% of the banks did not offer encrypted messaging for their clients who were given the opportunity to communicate to bank officers through email, and that 59% of the banks failed to give any warnings to their actual or potential clients as to the risks of sending unprotected messages via their websites.[34] These statistics suggest that the ease and convenience of communication between private banks and their clients have trumped security considerations for a number of banks. On the other hand, many of the leading Swiss banks provide risk warnings to customers when they use internet banking facilities, for example, warning clients that information concerning their transactions may be intercepted when transmitted over the internet, even if their information is encrypted.

The importance of the cybersecurity threat to financial systems is now being recognised by governments and regulators which have imposed new cybersecurity standards for corporations, especially banks, in dealing with client data. In 2018 the Swiss Federal Council adopted a national strategy to deal with cyber risks, while FINMA has revised its Circular 2008/21 concerning operational risks of banks. Under the revised Circular, financial institutions are subject to new risk management guidelines for handling the confidentiality of 'client-identifying data stored electronically'; at the same time, bank management is required to implement stringent cyber risk management standards, especially in relation to 'vulnerability assessments and penetration tests'.[35] Many countries, including Australia, have followed suit by creating prudential standards that require financial institutions to have rigorous security and control mechanisms specifically applicable to

---

security company who was responsible for transferring Swiss bank data between different branches of banks located in different countries, 15 December 2016.

33 Myprivatebanking, Privacy Vulnerability of Private Banking Websites, 4 March 2010, <http://www.myprivatebanking.com/article/myprivatebanking-research>.

34 Ibid. The survey of 195 websites in 17 major banking markets.

35 See Michael Isler, Jurg Schneider and Hugh Reeves, *Switzerland, Cybersecurity, Getting the Deal Through*, Law Business Research, London, February 2019.

commercial banks.[36] Whether banks will be prepared to make the human and technological investment to mitigate cybersecurity threats is a matter that will be keenly watched by regulatory authorities and analysts.

IV. Conclusions

The focus of this chapter has been on financial institutions. Although banks have generally improved the security of their computer systems, the same cannot be said for many professional groups, such as accountants, lawyers and trust and company service providers. According to a 2015 survey by the American Bar Association, 15 % of law firms in the United States 'have experienced a breach due to a hacker, website attack, physical break-in, or lost or stolen computer or smartphone' and, remarkably, less than 50% of those firms had any security response plan to deal with such breaches.[37] The implication of this is that financial information is and will continue to be vulnerable unless all those institutions and professions that store or have access to such data enact comprehensive security measures.

---

36 See Australian Prudential Regulation Authority, *Prudential Standard CPS 234 Information Security*, 2019.

37 See Booz Allen Hamilton, *Cyberthreats to Law Firms*, Executive Summary, 14 April 2016, https://www.boozallen.com/content/dam/boozallen/documents/2016/05/Cyberthreats%20to%20Law%20Firms_new_header.pdf.

Chapter 3

Startups and Legal Services in an Age of Digital Disruption

*Rod Henderson**

I have chosen two professional 'guilds' to carry out my public practice over 30 years as a tax adviser – I am both a solicitor and a chartered accountant. Throughout my career, I have been guided by an ethos I call 'tax acumen', helping clients without tax expertise make better business decisions through an 'after-tax' lens. I have left the big firm world of tax to pursue my personal interest in how disruptive technologies can more directly solve people's complex tax problems without always needing a professional adviser.

This has led me into the ecosystem of startups; more specifically, given my professional background, the fintech, regtech and legaltech startup communities. A world of 'robo advisers', 'free-docs', the 'gig economy' and 'freelancers'. To guide me on my way down the path to disruption, I have embarked on an immersion program; founding my own startup, locating myself in an innovation hub alongside other startup founders, meeting the players and stakeholders, mentoring emerging founders, investing in startups and conducting my own research on startups and disruption. I keep a daily digital log of this thoroughly enjoyable but challenging journey under the working title, 'The Startup Diary of a Late Starter'.

I have had the opportunity to work with the University of Sydney Business School to help develop a new practical capstone course for final-year

* The author expresses his appreciation to Associate Professor David Chaikin, Chair of the Discipline of Business Law, University of Sydney Business School, for his wise counsel and generous guidance, Dr Eva Huang, Lecturer in Business Law, University of Sydney Business School, for the opportunity to bounce ideas and provide challenge, and Ravi Nayyar, Research Assistant in the Discipline of Business Law, University of Sydney Business School, for his detailed and insightful editorial assistance.

students majoring in business law to help prepare them for the workforce. Drawing from my experiences in practice working with businesses, I am harnessing the concept of 'business law acumen' to guide business law students in solving legal problems to meet the practical needs of business. This brought me to focus on legal technology ('legaltech') startups that essentially are framed in response to the needs of users to obtain quick, easy to understand, low cost, practical and relevant legal solutions, ultimately by-passing the experts in the legal profession, at least until the users have a better understanding of their problems and needs. This also brings quality legal assistance in reach of those who cannot normally afford legal advice – a group I call 'the great unserviced'[1] – bringing access to justice for all.

On commencing work with the Business School, my very first question was what jobs in the legal sector do business law students take up now and, given the disruption of the professions, what jobs will be offered in the future? This nicely leads us into the topic of this paper – 'Startups and legal services in an age of digital disruption'. A business school is an ideal place to examine this topic. A business law student from a business school should be well-equipped to embark on a career in the new world of startups and legal services.

I. Disruption of the Law Versus Disruption of Legal Services

When we think about startups and the law, we can go down two main paths, as follows:

1. Disruption of the laws and regulation that govern us all: what I will not cover – the risks and opportunities that emerge as startups across all industries develop new business models to meet the needs of consumers by

---

1 Susskind refers to the 'latent legal market' as people who cannot afford to access traditional legal services: Richard Susskind, *Tomorrow's Lawyers: An Introduction to Your Future* (Oxford University Press, 2017) 128. Other terms include the 'missing middle' or 'low bono'.

pushing the boundaries of the existing protections, laws and conventions (e.g. music copyright, taxi regulation, financial planning and advice, banking, foreign exchange regulation, etc). This is a great and very large topic for another day.

2. Disruption of the legal profession and the delivery of legal services: what I will cover in this paper – the disruption of the conventional methods of delivery and the sources of legal expertise by new legaltech startups. This is achieved by automating legal processes, enabling laypeople to obtain a practical legal understanding of how the law applies to their circumstances as well as necessary legal documentation, and utilising digital solutions, including various forms of artificial intelligence ('AI').

Sectors prone to disruption are commonly dominated by monopolist-like players that may have naturally evolved (e.g. the four pillars of the Australian banks, the big four global accounting firms, etc). Statutory monopolies also provide fence-posts that have locked in business models and customer choice for decades, including taxi regulations, music copyrights and financial licenses. I might add that many of the regulations are there to protect consumers and suppliers alike. As business models evolve, however, quite rapidly in the age of digital disruption, business practices develop that outpace the development of the governing rules and regulations, and the underlying policy reasons for their existence (as will be illustrated shortly below in relation to the legal profession). Do the regulations protect consumers or simply the monopoly of the industry?

Professional bodies have been formed to protect a form of monopoly, the right to practice in a chosen field, similar to the trade guilds of medieval times. Sometimes protected by a Royal Charter and always governed by a code of conduct, such bodies are also characterised by strict admission criteria, ongoing quality-control compliance procedures, disciplinary action against non-compliant members and vigilant enforcement of the 'brand' to deter others from competing in the protected areas of practice.

For the legal profession in New South Wales, the Law Society of NSW forms the 'guild' which supports solicitors in practice and self-administers and regulates the rules of practice. This is backed up by the *Legal Profession Uniform Law 2014* (NSW) ('*LPUL*'), a form of statutory monopoly providing strong protection which ultimately prevents unqualified legal practitioners competing with solicitors. The underlying premise to justify this monopoly is that unqualified practitioners lack the necessary skill, experience and ethical oversight to service the needs of consumers.

Linking this to the themes of this conference, this paper will examine how, like any other 'protected' industry sector, the market for legal services is now open to disruption by entrepreneurs with new models, harnessing technology and fresh ways of thinking, and leading to the liberalisation of legal markets, disaggregation of the roles of a lawyer and the commoditisation of services. As we will see, this may involve a combination of:

- the disruption of the legal profession itself, as the statutory monopoly comes under pressure from new entrants, particularly as a result of the unbundling of components of the performance and delivery of legal services powered by new technologies (I call this 'external disruption'); and
- the disruption of roles and processes within the legal profession, caused by technological innovations in how legal work is performed and delivered within a legal practice or inhouse legal team ('internal disruption').

But ultimately, this paper seeks to bring the focus on the root cause of this disruption: the clients, their needs and their demand for value in how legal services are delivered to them.

II. Disruption of the Legal Profession
– The Science and Theory

Why are successful monopolies prone to be disrupted? Consistent with the principles espoused by Clayton Christensen in *The Innovator's Dilemma: When New Technologies Cause Great Firms to Fail* (Harvard Business Review Press, 1997), the more competent you are, the more exposed you are to disruption. Established businesses are 'held captive by their customers', their existing products and sources of revenue, and consequently routinely ignore emerging buyers who are not their customers. Why innovate when what you have is seemingly superior?

From personal experience, even within a highly innovative, established, professional services firm, it is challenging to introduce new processes or services that provide clients with a lower fee solution to an existing profitable service line. With some exceptions, such firms rarely 'give away' an answer to real problems but rather produce informative articles with 'hooks' to encourage enquiry to 'learn more'. Limited forms of innovative reinvention are provided with free apps and online bots. These are, however, generally little more than sales brochures and contact lists designed to generate 'leads' and do not solve a client's immediate problem.

Traditional firms are structured to provide a 'full-service' offering based on a long-term client relationship and repeat business which rewards the firm with annuity fee revenues. The value of the service delivered to clients is generally based on time and the hourly rate of the professionals, with the rate graduated by reference to the professional's skill and experience. Clients may not be able to justify the time and cost of engaging a professional firm, leading the client to act without professional assistance, which can lead to errors and costly mistakes. I believe that the number of clients in this category – the 'great unserviced' – is increasing as the cost of obtaining professional services continues to increase.

Professors Richard and Daniel Susskind, in *The Future of the Professions: How Technology Will Transform the Work of Human Experts*,[2] have taken a broader review across many professions, including lawyers, to examine 'How we share expertise in society?'. As the 'print-based industrial society' passes into history, in a 'technology-based Internet society', they:

> predict that increasingly capable machines, operating on their own or with no special users, will take on many of the tasks that have been the historic preserve of the professions. We anticipate an 'incremental transformation' in the way we produce and distribute expertise in society. This will lead eventually to the dismantling of the professions.[3]

In an earlier work, *The End of Lawyers?*[4], Professor Richard Susskind's detailed research suggests that traditional lawyers will, in a large part, 'be replaced by advanced systems, or by less costly workers supported by technology or standard processes, or by lay people armed with online self-help tools'.[5]

At the core of the Susskind theory is that the professions have enjoyed a unique 'social contract' or a 'grand bargain' which is simply becoming irrelevant in the technological age. In the case of lawyers, 'the principles underlying the exclusivity of lawyers are similar in most jurisdictions; and the pivotal justification is that it is in the clients' interests that those who advise them on the law are suitably trained and experienced'.[6]

In Table 1, I have sought to diagrammatically capture the essence of the Susskind 'theory of the commoditization' (*sic*) of professional work and why this is good for consumers. Applied to lawyers, it goes something like this:

---

3   Ibid 2.

4   Richard Susskind, *The End of Lawyers?* (Oxford University Press, 2017) 2.

5   In the US context, McGinnis and Pearce reach a similar view with the bold portent that 'Over time, machine intelligence will inevitably outperform human lawyers in completing most legal services': John O. McGinnis and Russell G. Pearce, 'The Great Disruption: How Machine Intelligence Will Transform the Role of Lawyers in the Delivery of Legal Services' (2014) 82 *Fordham Law Review* 3041, 3064.

6   Susskind and Susskind, above n 2, 22.

- The lawyers have already developed many processes in-house, initially standardised manually, such as their precedents library, that no longer require human bespoke expertise to be applied to each and every client problem. They simply use the same agreement used for a previous client and tailor a few variable details to match the new client's needs.

- Over the last twenty or so years, many processes have been internally systemised with digital solutions, including searching precedent data bases, external searches and document automation.

- With specialisation, the involvement of non-legally qualified experts and the assistance of technology, the construction of a legal solution is no longer solely the domain of a legally-qualified expert. Under the concept of disaggregation, a legal solution is broken down into components delivered by both legal practitioners and other experts, involving more than one firm, assisted by software tools.

- It is a relatively small step to externalise these internal stores of knowledge and systems, with pre-packaged online solutions to enable clients to directly access their own 'self-help' solutions. The lawyers face Christensen's innovator's dilemma:[7] the pathway to externalisation conflicts with their 'billable hours' business model – the greater human expertise and time required to complete a complex matter, the higher the fee reward. They hesitate due to a fear of cannibalising their own annuity fee base.

- While they hesitate, new entrants disrupt their business model and attract their clients to a new 'tech-driven' solution which is cheaper, faster and better.

---

7   Clayton Christensen, *The Innovator's Dilemma: When New Technologies Cause Great Firms to Fail* (Harvard Business Review Press, 1997).

- How? The commoditisation of legal services through technological innovation allows clients to receive a better quality, more certain and rapidly-delivered automated service, drawn from the input of many advisers and delivered at a higher volume to many users, enabling a lower cost to each customer. The digitisation of the collective expertise of many professionals, in the words of Professor Susskind, 'invariably outclasses even the most talented bespoke performance'.[8]

Table 1

The evolution of professional services

Susskind theory of the 'commoditization' of professional work

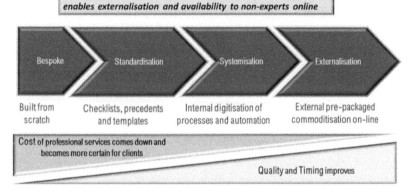

Disaggregation and digitisation of practical human expertise enables externalisation and availability to non-experts online

Bespoke	Standardisation	Systemisation	Externalisation
Built from scratch	Checklists, precedents and templates	Internal digitisation of processes and automation	External pre-packaged commoditisation on-line

Cost of professional services comes down and becomes more certain for clients

Quality and Timing improves

"The collective expertise of many professionals invariably outclasses even the most talented bespoke performance" Professor Richard Susskind Tomorrow's Lawyers

Source: Rod Henderson, AcuTax prepared 2018 based on *Tomorrow's Lawyers,* R.E. Susskind

These predictions, that we are rapidly experiencing in the marketplace today, are quite confronting for a legal professional or a student contemplating a future career in the law. Whilst I believe that the Susskind theory, developed over many years, is largely an accurate prediction of the

8   Susskind, above n 1, 31.

direction of professional services for many routine and common problems and eventually complex matters, my personal view is that much of the valuable function of a professional adviser is built around softer human skills embodied in the term 'trusted adviser'.

A trusted adviser's role is built around a relationship, aided by reputation from prior successes in simply helping clients solve problems and succeed in their business or personal endeavours. This does not require deep technical knowledge, though it requires an ability to access such expertise when required. This requires an ability to challenge and guide the client, particularly when the client does not know or understand their own problem. The 'human trusted adviser' relationship is enhanced by the technology and the commoditisation of professional services, as those two things allow the focus to be placed on helping the client achieve positive and successful outcomes to satisfy their known and unknown needs through the delivery of human and digitally enabled value. This value includes delivering a cost-effective solution. In other words, the human trusted adviser provides the 'unprogrammable' value.

The Susskind theory is playing a valuable role in jolting professionals to adapt and leverage the benefits of digital disruption and disaggregation of their vocations. Compared to a department of, say, 10 to 15 lawyers working in a specialist area of expertise in a law firm today, I have a vision of a much smaller 'client service team' of professionals of, say, one to two, which delivers the same level of output, for a similar fee reward and at a higher level of client satisfaction. They would service a much larger online client base, including clients who could not previously afford their services. This, so my vision goes, would be achieved with the support of a vast array of legal 'bots', automated systems, apps, data sources, external 'software as a service' (SaaS) providers, and unqualified non-lawyers. The cost of the services to each client will consequently fall with less lawyer time required to deliver a 'tech enabled' legal solution that, under the Susskind theory, costs less as it is drawn from the input of many advisers and delivered at a higher volume to many users. This will result in a larger and vibrant profession with a vast team of qualified and unqualified practitioners working with purpose, delivering value to solve the needs of many clients.

III. Legaltech Startups in Australia

Like other professions, the legal industry has been updating its practices with new technology to confront the challenges of the digital age, ultimately driven by the demands of clients and increasing competition for fee revenues.

The traditional law firms or 'BigLaw' (as Dr George Beaton refers to them) are striving to provide greater efficiencies through the use of technology as clients demand more value for those billable hours. 'NewLaw' comprises reinvented law firms and non-traditional entities such as virtual online or platform firms that are developing and adopting technology to change the aspects of 'how work is won and how work is done'[9].

Then we have the legaltech startups which nimbly challenge the traditional legal model by focusing on technology to create efficiencies both:

- within the law firms, including legaltech-delivered tools to enable internal disruption, such as the automatic delivery of legal services to clients; and
- directly for customers as legaltech startups act as external disruptors through, for example, the delivery of legal services and legal information by non-lawyers to customers.

Associated with the rise of the legaltech startups, we are seeing increased disaggregation, unbundling and the commoditisation of legal services that are leading to new ways in producing and delivering elements of the legal services. The emergence of disaggregation, and both internal disruption and external disruption is creating ethical and regulatory tensions within

---

9   George Beaton and Imme Kaschner, *Remaking Law Firms: Why and How* (American Bar Association, 2016).

the legal profession. These regulatory issues are examined under sections 4 and 5 below.

Table 2 illustrates the impact of digital innovation and disruption on the different 'players' within the legal profession:[10]

Table 2

Technology, innovation and disruption in the legal sector

Sector	Digital innovation	Level of disruption
BigLaw	Enablers, continuous improvements, automation, AI, blockchain, smart contracts, eConveyancing, practice management efficiencies	
NewLaw	Disaggregation, unbundling, network/platform firms, rent-a-lawyer, inhouse lawyers, gig-economy	
Legal Startups	Online legal information, commoditisation, free-docs and AI advice beyond legal services, non-lawyer disruptors	

Source: Rod Henderson AcuTax, 2017

As a contemporary reference, a selection of legaltech startups and sub-sectors in the Australian legaltech startup market are summarised in Table 3.

Table 3

Source: LawPath, August 2017, https://lawpath.com.au/blog/australian-legal-tech-startup-market-map

---

10 Rod Henderson, 'Startups and Legal Services in an Age of Digital Disruption' (Presentation, AcuTax, November 2017) Slide number 6.

A breakdown and description of the components of the above map is drawn from an article published by LawPath, a legaltech online legal services and document provider.[11]

IV. The Legal Profession's Response to Disruption of Legal Services

There is a feeling of injustice and unfairness within the legal profession. It costs money to run an active professional body and for members to have systems in place to ensure continued compliance with the strict quality-control requirements. As one of the NewLaw firms put it, 'law firms ... are competing with low-cost providers who escape regulation by denying that they are providing legal services, placing solicitors, who bear the economic cost of full compliance, at a competitive disadvantage'.[12]

Justice Daubney of the Queensland Supreme Court sees a professional lawyer as having higher ideals to meet too:[13]

> There is a palpable difference between carrying on or exercising the profession of the law, on the one hand, and carrying on the business of a lawyer, on the other. At least one of the hallmarks of the profession, apart from special skills and learning, is that the profession has *public service as its principal goal*. The distinction between a trade, business or occupation and a profession was described by Street CJ *in Re Foster* (1950) 50 SR (NSW) 149 at 151: 'A trade or business is an occupation or calling in which the primary object is the pursuit of pecuniary gain. Honesty and honourable dealing are, of course, expected from every man, whether he

---

11 Dominic Woolrych, *Australian Legal Tech Startup Market Map* (17 August 2017) LawPath <https://lawpath.com.au/blog/australian-legal-tech-startup-market-map>.

12 Law Society of New South Wales, 'Commission of Enquiry: FLIP Future of Law and Innovation in the Profession' (Report, Law Society of New South Wales, 2017) 101 ('FLIP Report').

13 *Legal Services Commissioner v Walter* [2011] QSC 132 (27 May 2011), [19] (Daubney J).

be engaged in professional practice or in any other gainful occupation. But in a *profession pecuniary success is not the only goal. Service is the ideal, and the earning of remuneration must always be subservient to the main purpose.*' [emphasis added]

With the higher cost of being a compliant solicitor and the lofty public service ideals laid down by Chief Justice Street in the 1950s and reaffirmed by Justice Daubney in 2011, how can solicitors financially continue to stay in practice if non-lawyers are allowed to effectively carry on the business of providing legal services under the guise of enabling customers to 'do it yourself' ('DIY') and by merely providing legal *information* rather than legal advice?

Proactively, the FLIP Report[14] provides a thorough state of play of the legal profession in the digital age, detailing the challenges and the attempts to find solutions to enable the professional to survive. The report's closing chapter, however, highlights that 'the regulation of the legal profession' contains a dire warning from a NewLaw contributing witness that 'consumers will go with who has got the best product, who is going to promise the quickest turnaround time, who's going to provide the best price – whether you're a law firm or not'.[15]

In the area of legal regulation, the FLIP Report lists a number of recommendations, including:

- investigation of bringing legal information within the regulatory fold;
- actively raising awareness among members of the public of the value of legal advice; and
- drafting guidance for lawyers to operate as entrepreneurs and businesses.

---

14 Law Society of New South Wales, above n 12.
   The Law Institute of Victoria released a similar study in 2015: Law Institute of Victoria, 'Disruption, Innovation and Change: The Future of the Legal Profession' (Report, Law Institute of Victoria, 2015).

15 Law Society of New South Wales, above n 12, 103.

The FLIP Report has moved into an implementation stage with a range of initiatives underway, and the Law Society and other contributors are to be commended for leading the way. Positively, the report keeps the client in focus and suggests that 'it is important that the regulatory touch continue to be light but judicious, serve the interests of the public, and foster innovation'.[16]

V. Are Legaltech Startups Legal?

Attempts to disrupt the legal profession are not new. For many years, accountants have been providing tax advice which some argue has been in breach of the legal practice laws, at least until tax advisers were given their own statutory monopoly to provide tax advice as 'tax agents' with the introduction of the *Tax Agent Services Act* 2009 (Cth). The relevant state-based law societies have successfully challenged many incursions into traditional areas of legal practice, such as in the Queensland Supreme Court case of *Legal Services Commissioner v Walter*,[17] where the respondent was found to have so closely engaged in the running of litigation matters that he had contravened the *Legal Profession Act* (Qld) by practicing law when he was not a qualified legal practitioner.

Enter the disruptors. With the advent of legaltech startups, as examined earlier in this chapter, new technologies and business models are beginning to eat into the relatively stable statutory monopoly enjoyed over many years by the legal profession. The traditional boundaries are becoming more uncertain as legaltech startups make incursions into areas where qualified lawyers generally practice: both within a law practice (internal disruption) and by competing with the services provided to clients by a law practice (external disruption). The legality of the services of legaltech startups under the LPUL[18] and its underlying rules and regulations is analysed in this chapter across the following boundary lines:

---

16 Ibid.

17 [2011] QSC 132 (27 May 2011) [19] (Daubney J).

18 *Legal Profession Uniform Law 2014* (NSW).

- the provision of legal services and advice by a qualified legal practitioner as qualified legal practice (QLP) v the unqualified practice of law (UPL) by legaltech startups;
- the provision of legal advice v legal information by legaltech startups; and
- the use of technology within a legal practice, powered by legaltech startups, to facilitate the provision of legal advice by 'robot lawyers' (e.g. automated document generation and other machine intelligence functions) v human lawyers.

A. *The Provision of Legal Services by an Unqualified Legal Practitioner*

In NSW, the legal profession finds statutory protection in section 10 of the LPUL[19] which prohibits the practice of law and the provision of legal services other than by a qualified Australian legal practitioner under pain of a penalty of $27,500 or imprisonment up to 2 years, or both. Like all things legal, the distinction comes down to the interpretation of the definitions including 'legal services' which means work done or business transacted in the ordinary course of legal practice. Unfortunately, 'legal practice' is not defined, other than in case law, leading to a somewhat circular interpretation ending in uncertainty.[20]

Looking through an 'old world' lens, the courts have been able to interpret whether a 'person' has been engaged in 'legal practice' or provided 'legal services' under older, but similar, legislation and associated case law in various states.[21] For example, 'if a person ... combines professing to be a solicitor with action usually taken by a solicitor – I think he then does act

---

19 Ibid.

20 Emma Beames, 'Technology-Based Legal Document Generation Services and the Regulation of Legal Practice in Australia' (2017) 42(4) *Alternative Law Journal* 297, 298.

21 Law Society of New South Wales, 'Practising in NSW under the Uniform Law: Unqualified Legal Practice' (Fact Sheet, Law Society of New South Wales, 2018).

as a solicitor'.[22] In *Legal Services Commissioner v Walter*,[23] there is a useful listing of the services that were found to 'lie near the very centre of the practice of litigation law', namely:

(a) advising parties to litigation in respect of matters of law and procedure;

(b) assisting parties to litigation in the preparation of cases for litigation;

(c) drafting court documents on behalf of parties to litigation;

(d) drafting legal correspondence on behalf of parties to litigation; and

(e) purporting to act as a party's agent in at least one piece of litigation.[24]

Looking through a 'new world' lens of disaggregation of the legal profession and the unbundling of legal services, the question now needs to be asked as to whether all the acts of 'advising', 'assisting', 'drafting' and 'acting' for a party are all acts carried on in the practice of law? Many tasks can be broken down and performed by the client, a pre-programmed computer, other experts and legaltech startups which each in themselves do not necessarily require the provision of legal services. Indeed, in *Legal Services Commissioner v Walter*,[25] Daubney J found that it was the 'combination' of services that contributed to his findings that the respondent unlawfully carried on the profession of law.[26]

Nonetheless, the Law Institute of Victoria has published 'Unqualified Practice Guidelines' that provide examples of actions that are legal services, taking a more prescriptive approach in an attempt to define the borderlines

---

22 *Re Sanderson; Ex parte The Law Institute of Victoria* [1927] VLR 394, 369 (Cussen J).

23 [2011] QSC 132 (27 May 2011).

24 *Legal Services Commissioner v Walter* 2011] QSC 132 (27 May 2011) [27] (Daubney J).

25 [2011] QSC 132 (27 May 2011).

26 Ibid [28] (Daubney J).

in the 'new world'. These include: preparation or drawing of documents of a legal nature, adapting a legal form or precedent to a particular case or exercising the mind as to what might be the appropriate form of words to use in a particular case for a third party.[27]

The Law Society of Western Australia has released a detailed position paper on *People Unlawfully Engaged in Legal Work: Protecting the Community* ('the WA paper').[28] Drawing out the simple example of the marketing of 'will kits', the WA paper looks at automated software used by financial planners to draft wills for clients without the testator meeting a solicitor. It cites the case of *Attorney General at the Relation of the Law Society of Western Australia v Quill Wills Ltd & Ors*[29] as 'an early example of non-lawyers using products to provide legal services to members of the public'. Noting that the case is now approaching 30 years old and was decided at a time long before the recent advancements in AI technology, it was held that the defendant had gone beyond 'merely giving abstract information as to legal rules and was assisting in the production of a will appropriate to the individual circumstances of the customer'.[30]

However, in the area of 'will kits' (which I believe have been around well before technology), the distinction is not entirely clear-cut as Heerey J said in the Federal Court in *Australian Competition and Consumer Commission v Murray*[31] under the heading, 'The boundaries of legal practice': '*It is common ground that the selling of will forms, with or without accompanying instructions and advice does not per se infringe statutory prohibitions of legal practice by non-lawyers. The question is whether the business promoted by the defendants went further and amounted to practising law*' (emphasis

---

27 Law Institute of Victoria Ethics, 'Unqualified Practice Guidelines' (Guidelines, Law Institute of Victoria Ethics, 2004) [2] <http://www.liv.asn.au/LIVPublicWebSite/files/d8/d893c45c-c95f-4745-b605-bf0a17cfe7f9.pdf>.

28 Law Society of Western Australia, 'People Unlawfully Engaged in Legal Work: Protecting the Community' (Position Paper, Law Society of Western Australia, 4 August 2017).

29 [1990] WASC 604 (27 November 1990).

30 Law Society of Western Australia, above n 28, 7.

31 [2002] FCA 1252 (11 October 2002).

added).[32] Ultimately, it was found that the wills business in that case constituted unlawful legal practice:

> The object of the licensee's attendance on that occasion was *not just the giving of abstract information as to legal rules, or the handing over of documents or forms*, but the production of a valid will appropriate to the individual circumstances of the customer: see *Dacey. This is the essence of legal practice, the advising of a particular person in a particular situation and the production of a document which affects legal rights and which is tailored to the particular needs of that person* [emphasis added].[33]

And, more recently in Western Australia, it was made clear in *Legal Practice Board v Giraudo*[34] that 'work of a merely clerical kind such as filling out blanks in a printed form or drawing instruments of a generally recognised type that does not involve the determination of the legal effect of special facts and conditions should not be regarded as legal work'.[35] Incidentally, this case did not involve technology and it was found that the very *human* actions of the defendant, in purporting to represent his client in proceedings and guiding the client in preparing documents, including the giving of legal advice, constituted unlawful legal practice.

Clearly, unqualified legaltech startups need to tread carefully. Many legaltech startups use well-crafted 'non-reliance' disclaimers and website terms and conditions, limiting the service to the delivery of 'legal information' rather than legal advice or legal practice. Usually, the legal information is reviewed and 'signed off' by a qualified lawyer or law firm. If it looks like advice from a solicitor, however, it may need to be provided by a qualified legal practitioner.[36]

---

32 Ibid [83] (Heerey J).

33 Ibid [94] (Heerey J).

34 [2010] WASC 4 (14 January 2010).

35 *Legal Practice Board v Giraudo* [2010] WASC 4 (14 January 2010) [13] (Hall J).

36 Beames, above n 20, 299 highlights that the statutory monopoly of legal practitioners cannot be simply displaced by disclaimers stating that the provider is not a

The WA paper briefly examines the online generation of legal documents at Section 9 – again touching on the example of 'will kits' and drawing upon anecdotal experiences about lack of appropriate insurance, lack of involvement of a lawyer 'between the time information is provided by the user and the final document is generated' – and concludes that 'All this could lead to a lack of protection for the public'.[37] This comes across as being somewhat disingenuous as it is the public which is demanding and using such services. Obviously, the public has a right to expect protection which they should receive under:

- the relevant State based legal profession laws and rules to ensure the lawyer acts ethically and competently and to prevent UPL;
- consumer protection laws for non-legal practice legal information services;
- relevant terms of engagement and disclosures of the service provider (whether they be a legal practitioner or otherwise); and
- insurances that are a necessary part of business, including professional indemnity ('PI') for legal practitioners and others, and cyber and IT insurance.

There are very good reasons for utilising the regulated services of a legal practitioner including (as noted at section 1 of the WA paper)[38] legal professional privilege and confidentiality, regulated PI insurance, regulated costs disclosures and agreements, trust accounts and, significantly, the code of professional conduct (including duties to avoid conflicts of interest); all of which, arguably, can only be legally provided by a qualified legal

---

lawyer and is not providing legal advice if in fact that is what they are doing, citing *Van Der Feltz v Legal Practice Board* [2017] WASC 2 (9 January 2017) [6] (Hall J) wherein it was found that the disclaimer 'I am not a Lawyer and do not give legal advice' did not alter the fact that litigation services were being provided.

37 Law Society of Western Australia, above n 28, 12.

38 Ibid 1.

practitioner. This is in addition to the experience and expertise certain solicitors can offer, though this is not the exclusive purvey of legal practitioners. As highlighted in the cases above, there are certain services of a legal nature (e.g. 'legal information') that do not constitute 'legal practice'.

i) The Provision of Legal Advice v Legal Information

There are certain types of 'standardised', common or commoditised, issues where the public (which includes sophisticated businesspeople, non-practicing lawyers, other professionals and lay people) simply does not see the value or need to engage a solicitor to produce DIY legal documents and forms unless, of course, the legal practitioner can provide this (legal information) service to the customer for a comparable price, quality and user experience. These public users do not require or want explanations or more detailed advice or guidance on the legal consequences of using the documents according to their circumstances.

The conclusion that can be drawn from much of the analysis is that there is a subtler distinction between QLP or legal advice v UPL v legal information. As found in a number of cases referenced above, the provision of forms and agreements delivered through an online automated document generation function with instructions and merely abstract information as to legal rules – to allow users to 'DIY' and add their own details, including names of parties, subject matters and dates, without advice as to the legal effectiveness and without addressing the individual circumstances of the customer – constitutes the delivery of legal information and should not constitute UPL. It follows that the provision of legal information and similar services by legaltech startups that do not involve the provision of legal advice should not constitute QLP. Information should not be assessed within the QLP v UPL divide.

It is questionable whether there is a need to 'investigate bringing legal information within the regulatory fold' as recommended by the FLIP Report. Being outside QLP, and not falling within UPL, I would suggest that legal information is primarily regulated by consumer protection laws. Being more precise, the area requiring greater regulatory focus and certainty is the outdated concept of legal practice in the modern digital age of disaggregation and the technological disruption of legal services.

ii) QLP v UPL – Regulatory Reforms and Where to From Here?

Regulatory reforms should be focused on how new technologies are redefining how legal services are delivered, including disaggregation, which is leading to lawyers and non-lawyers working together with technology to deliver legal solutions to benefit and meet the needs of clients or customers. This includes the ability of lawyers to rely on technology to automatically deliver components of legal advice and services. Invariably, as new business models emerge around these technologies, questions will be raised about whether the unqualified practice of the law is being conducted by non-lawyers or through the technologies they deploy. The regulatory boundary line still remains the age-old distinction of QLP v UPL.

A number of detailed papers have delved into the QLP v UPL distinction, including:

- in the US context, 'The Great Disruption: How Machine Intelligence Will Transform the Role of Lawyers in the Delivery of Legal Services' ('The Great Disruption')[39] uses the experience of the online document automation company, LegalZoom – which has been challenged for UPL in many US states – to conclude that 'machine intelligence has made significant progress in undermining lawyers' monopoly';[40]
- in the Australian context, the University of Melbourne Networked Society Institute's discussion paper, 'Current State of Automated Legal Advice Tools' (ALAT Paper), states that 'while public interest arguments can be raised

---

39 McGinnis and Pearce, above n 5.

40 Ibid 3059.

against unqualified practice of law (UPL) controls, it is not in the public interest that access to public legal information be circumscribed in support of professional monopoly privileges';[41] and

- the Law Institute of Victoria's paper, 'Disruption, Innovation and Change: The Future of the Legal Profession', canvases softer regulatory approaches, including taking 'into account whether an innovation is consistent with the purpose and objectives of the regulation, even where it fails to comply with the letter of the regulatory rules'.[42]

Redefining the definition and practical boundaries of QLP (and, therefore, UPL) is where all the papers and commentators (especially McGinnis and Pearce, Susskind and the Networked Society Institute at the University of Melbourne) converge, which the ALAT paper perhaps ably sums up best with:

A recent report (IBA, 2016) has suggested that the evolution of legal services from bespoke to commoditised and standardised or packaged services with the aid of ALATs [Automated Legal Advice Tools] 'are likely to yield significant benefits for consumers in terms of cost, quality and access to justice' (IBA, 2016, p. 5). This may require lawyers to 'overcome the conservative, risk-adverse culture that seems to pervade the profession and may need to deconstruct their structure and pricing models (IBA, 2016, p. 5).[43]

41 Networked Society Institute, University of Melbourne, 'Current State of Automated Legal Advice Tools' (Discussion Paper No 1, Networked Society Institute, University of Melbourne, 2018) 30.

42 The Law Institute of Victoria, 'Disruption, Innovation and Change: The Future of the Legal Profession' (Report, The Law Institute of Victoria, 2015) 35.

43 Networked Society Institute, University of Melbourne, above n 41, 31, quoting IBA Legal Policy & Research Unit, International Bar Association, '"Times are a-Changin": Disruptive Innovation and the Legal Profession' (Report, IBA Legal

'Deconstruction' of existing definitions and boundaries of QLP is vital for solicitors to remain relevant and to lead the delivery of legal solutions to benefit clients in the digital age, working constructively with non-lawyers and technology. Regulation needs to be dynamic with a process to streamline necessary updates, together with a principles-based approach to allow interpretations to evolve, assisted by proactive regulators through the issue of fact sheets and other guidance on emerging issues.

B. AI and the Solicitor's Code of Conduct to Act Competently

The discussion above has focused on the distinction as to whether the provider of the legal services is qualified, or not, as a legal practitioner. A subsidiary question is whether the automated provision of legal advice by AI, within a legal practice, could constitute a breach of the solicitors' code of conduct to act competently in the best interests of a client. In particular, rule 4.1.3 of the *Legal Profession Uniform Law Australian Solicitors' Conduct Rules 2015* (NSW), states that a solicitor 'must deliver legal services competently, diligently and as promptly as reasonably possible'. Rule 7.1, 'Communication of advice', states that 'a solicitor must provide clear and timely advice to assist a client to understand relevant legal issues and to make informed choices about action to be taken during the course of a matter, consistent with the terms of the engagement'.[44] This requires a consideration of the legality of the use of 'robot lawyers' v human lawyers within a legal practice that is carrying on QLP.

In examining the provisions of commoditised or unbundled services, the FLIP Report recognises that there is no prohibition against a legal practitioner conducting work pursuant to a limited scope retainer under the LPUL. But the report highlights there are risks to lawyers that need to

---

Policy & Research Unit, International Bar Association, May 2016) 5.

44 The use of AI raises broader more elevated ethical issues above the mere practice of law. For example, the European Parliament proposes the enactment of robot law in Europe – refer the Committee on Legal Affairs, European Parliament, 'Report with Recommendations to the Commission on Civil Law Rules on Robotics' (Report No A8-0005/2017, Committee on Legal Affairs, European Parliament, 27 January 2017).

be carefully navigated, referring to the requirement under section 174(3) of the *Legal Profession Uniform Law 2014 (NSW)* for the solicitor to take all reasonable steps to satisfy itself that the client has understood and given consent to the proposed course of action for the conduct of the matter.[45] Accordingly, the conclusion can be drawn that solicitors can provide automated advice and legal services to clients under a limited scope retainer, provided the cost agreements clearly explains the nature and limitations of the services (e.g. the deliverable is focused on specific issues and does not consider the whole range of legal issues that might be relevant to the client) and the solicitor obtains their client's consent. The FLIP Report recommends, however, that protection for solicitors be made unambiguous by statutory amendment.[46] The NSW FLIP Report also acknowledges that the ethical questions of AI-supported advice need to be more closely researched and refers to work conducted overseas as a starting point.[47]

In the US, the thinking and regulatory direction is quite advanced. McGinnis and Pearce conclude, based on updates to the ABA (American Bar Association) Model Rules, that lawyers can ethically use the services of non-lawyer firms that rely on machine intelligence 'so long as the lawyer makes reasonable efforts to ensure that the services are provided in a manner that is compatible with the lawyer's professional obligations' which includes the lawyer controlling and 'supervising' the input of such machine intelligence services.[48] In response to concerns whether lawyers have the requisite technical knowledge to supervise such vendors, the US ABA Model Rule of Professional Conduct 1.1 was updated in 2012 to include Comment 8: 'To maintain the requisite knowledge and skill, a lawyer should keep abreast of changes in the law and its practice,

---

45 Law Society of New South Wales, above n 12, 102 and see note 7 of Chapter 10 of that report.

46 Ibid 102. Further work has been conducted by the FLIP research stream on the ethical implications of the provision of limited scope services by lawyers, refer Michael Legg, 'Recognising New Forms of Legal Practice: Limited Scope Services' (2018) (50) *LSJ* 74.

47 Ibid 41–2, 102–3.

48 McGinnis and Pearce, above n 5, 3060.

including the *benefits and risks associate with relevant technology* [emphasis added]'.[49]

Similar updates should be considered in Australia to the LPUL[50] and associated rules to keep pace with technology and changing practices to provide some definition to the boundaries in allowing 'robot lawyers' (e.g. automated document generation and other machine intelligence functions), within a legal practice to, in effect, internally disrupt human lawyers. The acid test for this strand might be whether an online legaltech software service can be ethically used under the LPUL in Australia by a legal practice to:

- allow a client with a particular legal problem to find the law firm's legal solution online;
- enter into a solicitor's electronically signed cost agreement which the client signs electronically or selects 'agree' online, including making disclosures to and obtaining consents from the client as to the manner in which the advice is being delivered with the use of AI;
- obtain details about the client and their problem through an interactive automated question and information-gathering function;
- assemble and issue the completed document which is tailored to the client's individual circumstances (with the solicitor's e-signature attached); and
- do all of the above with no direct contact between the client and any human?

Has the solicitor acted competently, as required by rule 4.1.3 of the *Legal Profession Uniform Law Australian Solicitors' Conduct Rules 2015* (NSW) and met the obligation to communicate advice in a manner which

---

49 Sandra R. McCandless and Stephen Klein, 'Ethical Issues Posed by Artificial Intelligence' (Report, Dentons US, 16 January 2018).

50 *Legal Profession Uniform Law 2014* (NSW).

assists the client to understand relevant legal issues and to make informed choices about action to be taken during the course of the matter (e.g. under rule 7.1)? Can we say 'yes', provided the 'responsible solicitor' has prepared and reviewed the content and inputs, 'supervised' and reviewed the preparation of the automation software and conducted regular checks, thereby 'ensuring that the services are provided in a manner that is compatible with the lawyer's professional obligations'?[51] The wording of the costs agreement is important too, as examined earlier in relation to limited scope retainers.

Similar to the ABA Model Rules in the US, further rules need to be developed in Australia to provide legal practitioners with guidance and certainty on how they can ethically apply technology to automate a range of services utilising the software of legaltech startups and other non-lawyer experts. This should include requiring lawyers to be proficient in understanding relevant technologies.[52] With the rapid pace at which clients and customers are turning to disruptive technologies to meet their legal needs, this is critical to the survival of the profession.

VI. Risks and Opportunities in a Disaggregated Market

Whilst there are many opportunities for users of legal services and for the startups that fill this gap, of course, there are risks, including a 'dumbing down' of the quality of legal solutions, threats to the 'sanctity' of the law and the making of outright errors resulting in losses and damages to users. A selection of risks and opportunities from the disruption of the legal services market is listed in Table 4.

---

51 McGinnis and Pearce, above n 5, 3047.

52 The FLIP Report suggests guidance and continuing education for lawyers in areas of technology relevant to the delivery of competent legal services: Law Society of New South Wales, above n 12, 42.

**Table 4. Risks and Opportunities of Disruption
of the Legal Services Market**

Risks	Opportunities
Subject matter experts and specialists 'die out'	Career path for business law graduates
'Dumbing down' of legal advice	Clients align legal and business needs
Lack of nuanced empathy and intuition	Employment with legaltech startups
Loss of experience and quality	'Unprogrammable' value of the trusted adviser
Bespoke advice only for the wealthy	Crowdfunded class advice/crowdsourcing advice
Unemployed and low-paid lawyers	24/7 immediate online answers to legal problems
Loss of legal professional privilege	Low-cost DIY legal documents
'Slipping through the cracks' with loss & damages to clients UPL not covered by PI insurance	New jobs created – legal SaaS, legal IT risk, legal customer support and legal knowledge engineers
Clients 'don't know what they don't know' when selecting problems they should solve themselves	Superior collective expertise enhances quality of legal advice
Over reliance on 'the machines'	Affordable access to justice
Lawyers not understanding the technology	Targeted bespoke services for complex problems
The profession moves too late	Client receives value

Source: Rod Henderson AcuTax, 2017

Controversial and often polarising legal professionals, the ultimate conclusion of the Susskind theory is a lawyerless future with professionals pushed aside by the ascendancy of robots, systems, software and unqualified service providers. Susskind offers future lawyers two career choices: to either *compete* with the machines or *build* the machines.[53] Whether the reader agrees or not, this paper's objective is to help readers gain an appreciation of how the legal profession is being rapidly disrupted by the demands of users in the market, with many emerging issues, risks and opportunities still to play out. The good of all this is a re-focusing on the client's needs. As my old firm's mission statement put it, 'We exist to turn our knowledge into value for the benefit of our clients'.[54]

My vision for the future is that we will witness a convergence. In time, BigLaw will adapt to the disruptive impacts on their business models, providing streamlined limited retainer technology-enabled services where, for example, their larger clients have the competency to perform legal tasks internally. NewLaw will establish a role servicing certain needs of traditional clients of BigLaw. Legaltech startups will flourish servicing both law firms and users directly. Modernisation of professional ethical regulatory rules to guide the use of technology will accelerate these changes and provide greater certainty for both qualified legal practitioners, and unqualified providers of information and software. This will enable people to solve their own legal problems, including the 'great unserviced' who cannot afford traditional legal advice. Ultimately whether the legal service is delivered as legal advice or legal information, disruptive technologies will find their natural place as *enablers* to enhance the client's needs and satisfy the client's continuing demand for value.

---

53 Susskind, above n 1, 188.
54 KPMG Mission Statement, referenced by Susskind, above n 1, 189–90.

Chapter 4

Insider Trading and Technology

Juliette Overland

Technological developments are changing the ways in which we communicate, access information, and carry out a variety of commercial activities. This paper considers the ways in which those technological developments are having an impact on insider trading. The use of technology has significant implications for those who may be tempted to engage in insider trading, as well as those who wish to detect insider trading and enforce insider trading laws and presents a variety of challenges in need of resolution and clarity.

I. What Is Insider Trading?

Insider trading is prohibited under s 1043A(1) of the *Corporations Act 2001* (Cth) (the '*Corporations Act*'), which provides:

> Subject to this subsection, if:
>
> (a) a person (the insider) possesses inside information; and
>
> (b) the insider knows, or ought reasonably to know, that the matters specified in paragraphs (a) and (b) of the definition of inside information in section 1042A are satisfied in relation to the information;[1]

---

1   Section 1042A of the *Corporations Act* provides that 'inside information' means information in relation to which the following paragraphs are satisfied:
(a) the information is not generally available; and
(b) if the information were generally available, a reasonable person would expect it to have a material effect on the price or value of particular Division 3 financial products.

the insider must not (whether as principal or agent):

(c) apply for, acquire or dispose of, relevant Division 3 financial products, or enter into an agreement to apply for, acquire, or dispose of, relevant Division 3 financial products; or

(d) procure another person to apply for, acquire, or dispose of, relevant Division 3 financial products, or enter into an agreement to apply for, acquire, or dispose of, relevant Division 3 financial products.[2]

Insider trading can therefore be broadly described as having four main elements:

(i)   a person possesses certain information;

(ii) the information is inside information – that is, that it is not generally available information, but if it were it would be likely to be material in relation to certain financial products;

(iii) the person knows (or ought reasonably to know) that the information is inside information; and

(iv) while in possession of the information, the person trades in relevant financial products, procures another person to do so, or communicates the information to another person likely to do so.

---

2   There is an additional prohibition in s 1043A(2) of the *Corporations Act*, which provides that an insider must not:
>   directly or indirectly, communicate the information, or cause the information to be communicated, to another person if the insider knows, or ought reasonably to know, that the other person would or would be likely to:
>   (d) apply for, acquire, or dispose of, relevant Division 3 financial products, or enter into an agreement to apply for, acquire, or dispose of, relevant Division 3 financial products; or
>   (e) procure another person to apply for, acquire, or dispose of, relevant Division 3 financial products, or enter into an agreement to apply for, acquire, or dispose of, relevant Division 3 financial products.

II. What Has Technology Changed for Potential Insider Traders?

Advances in technology have impact for potential insider traders, in relation to the manner and ease in which they may be able to access inside information, to communicate with co-offenders and co-conspirators, and to engage in trading activity.

A. Manner and Ease of Access to Information

Access to the internet, and the ubiquity of smartphones and other personal devices, enables all of us to access more information than ever before, more easily than ever before. However, most of the information which we are able to access via the internet is in the public domain, making it 'readily observable' and therefore 'generally available' within the meaning of s 1042C of the *Corporations Act*,[3] with the result that it is not inside information. A consequence of the availability of a mass of information is that it becomes more difficult to thoughtfully analyse all the information which can be accessed. While investment banks and research analysts are able to devote significant time and resources to the analysis and systematic evaluation of all available information relevant to particular companies or sectors, such a task is increasingly beyond the scope and ability of regular investors.

The sheer volume of information which is available can also make the requirement to prove that information was not 'generally available',

---

3   The term 'generally available' is also defined in s 1042C of the *Corporations Act*, which provides that information is generally available if:
(a) it consists of readily observable matter; or
(b) both of the following subparagraphs apply:
(i) it has been made known in a manner that would, or would be likely to, bring it to the attention of persons who commonly invest in Division 3 financial products of a kind whose price might be affected by the information; and
(ii) since it was made known, a reasonable period for it to be disseminated among such persons has elapsed; or
(c) it consists of deductions, conclusions or inferences made or drawn from either or both of the following:
(i) information referred to in paragraph (a);
(ii) information made known as mentioned in subparagraph (b)(i).

which is in essence a requirement to prove a negative, a Herculean feat. Rumours spread much more quickly over the internet, information is more easily shared, and the ability to demonstrate that information was or was not in the public domain becomes ever more difficult. Additionally, with so much information able to be accessed, it can be difficult to establish precisely which piece of information is 'material'. This task is made more difficult when analysing a number (sometimes a great number) of pieces of information which alone would not be material, but when combined have a 'mosaic' effect of influencing those who would ordinarily trade in financial products.[4] This increasingly leads to the need for expert evidence as to whether certain information was generally available, and whether it was likely to be material, as shown in the recent case of *R v Noske*,[5] instead of those issues being determined by a jury.

B. Hacking and Cybercrime

Technology also enables organisations and businesses to store vast quantities of information. While we may have previously viewed insider traders as those who are true insiders, with an employment or other professional connection to the relevant company whose financial products are affected, or those who come across inside information fortuitously but unexpectedly, technology increasingly enables 'outsiders' to seek out and obtain inside information. As a result, 'hackers' are increasingly likely to target the information stored by organisations and businesses in an attempt to acquire inside information for the specific purpose of engaging in insider trading. In May 2017, a Ukrainian hacker was sentenced to two and a half years in prison for his role in a conspiracy to conduct insider trading based on stolen corporate news released prior to their publication, with related charges against 40

---

4   In the US, 'mosaic theory' requires consideration as to whether the addition of a particular piece of information substantially alters the nature of the total mix of information available: *Basic, Inc. v. Levinson*, 485 U.S. 224, 231–2 (1988); *TSC Indus., Inc. v. Northway, Inc.*, 426 U.S. 438, 449 (1976).

5   *R v Noske* [1987] WASC 56 (8 March 2017).

other defendants.[6] In September, the US Securities Exchange Commission (SEC) revealed that it had been targeted again by hackers seeking access to non-public information for insider trading purposes.[7] Other organisations that hold confidential, commercially sensitive information, may also find themselves the subject of such attacks from cyber-criminals eager to exploit any information they can access.

C. Communication Between Co-conspirators

Technology changes the ways in which co-conspirators and co-offenders can communicate and share inside information, or details of their trading activities, with a vast array of technological platforms that can be used for this purpose. Last year, in *R v Curtis*[8] evidence was produced about the blackberry 'pinning' methods which Curtis and his co-conspirator used to pass information about the contracts-for-difference (CFDs) in which they wished to trade, in an effort to avoid detection. While communicating and sharing information by email and other more easily traceable methods may assist regulators to gather evidence, as will be discussed below, insider traders are increasingly able to use technology to communicate secretively and privately.

D. High Frequency Trading

Advances in technology have changed the ways in which securities trading occurs. The heady days of the exchange trading floor are long since over, with trading occurring primarily online. The increasingly automated nature of securities trading has also given rise to high frequency trading. High frequency trading occurs via the use of algorithms to analyse information,

---

6   'Ukrainian hacker gets prison in U.S. insider trading case', *Reuters*, 23 May 2017, <https://www.reuters.com/article/us-trading-cyber-plea/ukrainian-hacker-gets-prison-in-u-s-insider-trading-case-idUSKBN18I2DF>.

7   'US SEC says hackers may have traded using stolen insider information', *Reuters*, 21 September 2017, <https://www.reuters.com/article/legal-us-sec-intrusion/u-s-sec-says-hackers-may-have-traded-using-stolen-insider-information-idUSKCN-1BW1K0>.

8   *R v Curtis (No 3)* [2016] NSWSC 866.

market movements, and to create and process trading orders, which occur within fractions of a second. This enables a trader to act before an ordinary investor could conceivably digest and respond to relevant information. High frequency trading also creates many more trades on the market than were previously possible. While this form of trading is certainly not illegal, the vast number of trades it generates make it more difficult to observe and monitor the market, which is an added complication in the detection and identification of suspicious trading. When those who legally trade via high frequency trading are able to respond almost instantaneously to the small market movements which may result from insider trading, it makes those initial insider traders that much harder to detect. Additionally, it has the potential, like insider trading,[9] to impact on market confidence and therefore market integrity, as ordinary investors are increasingly likely to form the view that they cannot compete with those who are able to engage in high frequency trading activities.

III. What Has Technology Changed for Regulators?

Advances in technology also have implications for regulators, who have increased tools available to detect insider trading, and to gather evidence of illegal activity.

A. Detection of Insider Trading

Since October 2013, the Australian securities market regulator, the Australian Securities and Investments Commission (ASIC) has been using a real-time market surveillance system, known as Flexible Advanced

---

9   Insider trading is prohibited on the basis that it harms market integrity, due to its impact on market confidence and market fairness: Standing Committee on Legal and Constitutional Affairs, House of Representatives, *Fair Shares for All: Insider Trading in Australia* (1989), [3.34]–[3.36]; ASIC, Consultation Paper 68 '*Competition for Market Services – Trading in Listed Securities and Related Data*' (2007); Utpal Bhattacharya and Hazem Daouk, 'The World Price of Insider Trading' (2002) 57 *Journal of Finance* 75; Laura Nyantung Beny, 'Insider Trading Laws and Stock Markets Around the World: An Empirical Contribution to the Theoretical Law and Economics Debate' (2007) 32 *Journal of Corporation Law* 237; *Mansfield & Kizon v R* (2012) 87 ALJR 20.

Surveillance Technologies (FAST) which uses sophisticated algorithms to detect unusual trading and market activity – it may be based on an unusual volume of trades, an unusual rise or fall in securities prices, or other unusual trading patterns. Unlike previous systems which only gave oversight via broker trades, the system enables individual investors to be monitored, and give rise to multiple daily alerts of suspicious trading.

Interestingly, it appears that information received via tipoffs and from whistleblowers remains an important contribution to the detection of insider trading, and this has been demonstrated in a number of recent cases.[10] This does seem to indicate, perhaps somewhat surprisingly, that technological advancements do not appear to have replaced traditional detection mechanisms. Of course, tipoffs and information from whistleblowers may confirm existing suspicions of unlawful conduct which otherwise would be difficult to act upon. However, once suspected insider trading has been detected, an investigation can be launched, and it is in this area that the use of technology is making a significant difference.

B. Obtaining Evidence of Insider Trading

Once an investigation for suspected insider trading has begun, technology provides additional means of gathering evidence to prove the misconduct. The sophistication of the offender will impact on how easy or difficult a task that may be. Offenders who communicate by email, and easily traced methods of communication, may provide a variety of digital footprints that make the gathering of evidence against them easier. For example, it was reported earlier this year that an academic at MIT was charged with insider trading after searching online for tips for engaging in insider trading.[11] However, more technologically sophisticated offenders are likely to make strenuous efforts to avoid detection and to take steps to minimise evidential opportunities.

---

10 See, for example, *Commonwealth Director of Public Prosecutions v Hill and Kamay* [2015] VSC 86; *R v Curtis (No 3)* [2016] NSWSC 866.

11 Alleged insider trader caught after googling 'insider trading', CNBC, 13 July 2017, <https://www.cnbc.com/2017/07/13/alleged-insider-trader-caught-after-googling-insider-trading.html>.

It has been noted by the Treasury[12] that ASIC has observed there have been changes in the platforms by which corporate criminals communicate (including internet-based messaging platforms such as Snapchat, WeChat and WhatsApp). These internet text-based and 'voice over internet protocol' communications are not captured by stored communication or telecommunication data warrants. They can only be detected using telecommunication interception.

As part of the ASIC Enforcement Review, the Treasury recently invited submissions on whether ASIC should become a 'recipient agency' so that it can receive telecommunications intercept material lawfully obtained by interception agencies.[13] If enacted, this would increase ASIC's ability to gather relevant evidence, which is something which US counterparts credit as essential in the enforcement of insider trading laws.[14]

In this context, the storage of metadata by communications service providers, and the use to which that metadata can be put, has the potential to make a significant impact on the enforcement of insider trading laws. Records of communications activity can be particularly useful, even if the content of that activity is not known or available. For example, evidence that certain people sent texts to each other on certain days, and at certain times of the day, may be particularly useful if it can be linked to the timing of particular trading activity – the actual content of the texts may not even be necessary. Again, the ease with which evidence of insider trading can be obtained as a result of an offender's digital footprint or metadata records

---

12 Treasury ASIC Enforcement Review, Positions and Consultation Paper 5, *ASIC's Access to Telecommunications Intercept Material*, July 2017, 17.

13 The case of *R v Cantena* (2012) 273 FLR 469 demonstrated some of the difficulties that can exist when attempting to use recorded telephone calls as evidence in insider trading proceedings in Australia.

14 Preet Bharara (former US Attorney for the Southern District of New York), 'The Future of White Collar Enforcement: A Prosecutor's View' (Speech delivered at the New York City Bar Association, New York, 20 October 2010); Preet Bharara, as quoted by Zachary Goldfarb, 'Insider Trading Ensnares Six: Prosecutors Accuse Hedge Fund Manager, Others of Raking in $20 million' *Washington Post*, 17 October 2009, and noted in Kenneth M Breen and Sean T Haran, 'The Rise of Wiretaps and Government Eavesdropping in Securities Fraud Cases' (2011) 35 *Champion* 33.

will depend on the sophistication, preparation and technical ability of that offender.

IV. Ongoing Challenges

When considering the issues that technology presents in relation to insider trading, there are a number of ongoing challenges which are worthy of further attention and analysis.

A. What Is the Impact of Digital Currencies?

Technology has enabled the creation and use of digital currencies, also known as 'cryptocurrencies', which do not exist in a physical form. Bitcoin is a popular example of a digital currency. Digital currencies are not legal tender, so they can only be used as a form of currency if another person is willing to accept them. They can be bought or sold on online exchange platforms and are commonly used for online transactions, although special ATMs for Bitcoins are now appearing across Australia, and in other countries. The increasing use and popularity of digital currencies raises a number of regulatory issues, including whether they are a financial product to which insider trading laws apply.

The Senate Economics References Committee report 'Digital currency – game changer or bit player?', released in August 2015, primarily recommended a 'wait and see' approach to the regulation of digital currencies. In that report, the Committee accepted ASIC's view that digital currencies do not fall within the current definition of financial products under the *Corporations Act*.[15] The insider trading prohibition applies to 'Division 3 financial products'[16] so, as a result, the insider trading prohibition would

---

15 Senate Economics References Committee, *Digital currency – game changer or bit player?*, August 2015, 8.

16 Section 1042A of the *Corporations Act* states that 'Division 3 financial products' means:

    (a) securities; or

    (b) derivatives; or

    (c) interests in a managed investment scheme; or

not apply to trading in digital currencies. However, ASIC has noted that derivatives offered over digital currency will amount to financial products.[17] This will have the consequence that the insider trading prohibition will apply to trading in those digital currency derivatives, expanding the gamut of financial products in which insider trading can occur, and increasing those for which regulatory oversight is required.

B. Cyber-security and the Management of Confidential Information

As a result of the increase in 'hacking' in order to try to gain access to inside information, greater emphasis is likely to be placed on the need for cyber-security in order to protect confidential information. Current practice for businesses and their advisers undertaking sensitive transactions is to require the relevant parties to sign non-disclosure agreements, agreeing to keep relevant information confidential. While this practice will no doubt continue, it needs to be recognised that information stored electronically about the transaction may be vulnerable to hackers seeking to access it for the purpose of insider trading. When a non-disclosure agreement contains a standard obligation to take reasonable steps to ensure that information cannot be accessed by other parties, it might be argued that there is a positive obligation to ensure that reasonable steps are taken to ensure that any system on which the information may be stored is not vulnerable to hacking or other unauthorised access. Therefore, the security of the technology used by the relevant parties and their organisations may be subject to scrutiny in this context.

(ca) debentures, stocks or bonds issued or proposed to be issued by a government; or

(d) superannuation products, other than those prescribed by regulations made for the purposes of this paragraph; or

(e) any other financial products that are able to be traded on a financial market.

17 ASIC, Senate inquiry into digital currency – Submission by the Australian Securities and Investments Commission, 15.

C. *The Knowledge Element of Insider Trading*

The 'knowledge element' of insider trading requires proof that the alleged offender knew, or ought reasonably to have known, that the relevant information was not generally available, and that, if it were, the information would be likely to be material. This element has long been considered to be one of the most difficult to prove and one of the greatest impediments to the enforcement of insider trading laws.[18] While the use of technology may assist in the gathering of evidence to support a prosecution, it appears unlikely to resolve the difficulties associated with proof of the knowledge element in connection with sophisticated offenders.

V. Conclusions

As technological developments continue to change the ways in which we are able to communicate, access information, and engage in a variety of commercial activities, the impact on corporate crimes like insider trading will evolve. There are clearly advantages and disadvantages for both potential insider traders and regulators resulting from the changing use of technology and impact of 'big data'. While traditional methods of detection and enforcement remain important tools to be utilised as appropriate, an increased adaptability, vigilance and a willingness to gain an understanding of the role of technology in corporate crime, are required in order to fight the ongoing battles against insider trading.

---

18 Explanatory Memorandum, Financial Services Bill 2001 (Cth), [2.78]–[2.79]; CAMAC, *Insider Trading Report*, (2003), [2.139]; Roman Tomasic, *Casino Capitalism? Insider Trading in Australia* (Australian Institute of Criminology, 1991) 115–26. It has been noted by the former Chair of ASIC, Alan Cameron, 'proving that a person had knowledge is often harder than it sounds unless there is smoking-gun type of evidence': Alan Deans, 'The Fetter of the Law', *The Bulletin*, 28 November 2000, 52; Simon Rubenstein, 'The Regulation and Prosecution of Insider Trading in Australia: Towards Civil Penalty Sanctions for Insider Trading' (2002) 20 *Company and Securities Law Journal* 89, 106.

Chapter 5

Panel Discussion: Insider Trading, Continuous Disclosure and Securities Trading Policies: Are They Effective from an Executive Perspective?

Panel chair:
- *Associate Professor Juliette Overland, University of Sydney Business School*

Panel members:
- *Ms Rachel Launders, General Counsel and Company Secretary, Nine Entertainment Co. Holdings Ltd*
- *Mr Dominic Millgate, Company Secretary, Boral Ltd*
- *Mr Matt Egerton-Warburton, Special Counsel, King & Wood Mallesons*

Assoc. Prof. Overland: The panel has been assembled today to discuss the interrelated topics of insider trading, continuous disclosure and securities trading policies. Our panellists will be asked to consider, not only the purely legal aspects of these issues, but the practical, everyday ramifications of these requirements on businesses. Given the types of roles our panellists hold within their respective companies, our discussion will focus on their personal experiences of effective and ineffective ways of implementing these regulatory requirements.

To begin our discussion, I would like to start with an introductory statement regarding the intersection of these three types of regulation. Insider trading laws, as I will discuss later in my presentation, are designed to maintain market integrity by making it unlawful for people who have inside information to trade themselves, procure others to trade on their behalf, or to tip that information to another person who they ought reasonably believe may trade. With regards to securities trading policies and continuous disclosure, such regulatory obligations are placed on listed companies so that if they become aware of price sensitive, non-public information, they are obliged to the tell the ASX in order to keep the market informed. The onus is placed on the organisations themselves to inform the market of any such information so that share prices are more accurate. Companies are also obliged to maintain securities trading policies, as a condition of being listed on the exchange. These policies create either blackout periods or trading windows within which employees, executives and key management personnel are restricted from trading in that company's securities. Such policies will set out processes and procedures for employees, executives and others to obtain clearance prior trading in the company's securities. These procedures are primarily implemented for two reasons. First, to limit opportunities for insider trading. Second, to ensure that persons external to the company have confidence that those within the company, who are likely to possess inside information because of their roles, have restrictions placed around when they can trade in that company's securities. To begin our discussion, I would like to ask Rachel Launders and Dominic Millgate, as company secretaries within their respective organisations, whether they both agree with the summary I have just given of how these three sets of regulations intercept.

Ms Launders: I think yes, broadly, I would agree with you. I think that the three pieces fit together quite nicely to form a framework and I do think the three pieces do work together in a triangulated way to support each other. For me, the largest concern is around continuous disclosure and internally making sure that those in an organisation, who should not be trading are not trading. I believe that having strong insider trading laws, that we see being enforced, can be a helpful reminder for staff that if they go off the rails, if they do not do the right thing, they are potentially going to end up in quite a lot of trouble. So, I actually think the framework works quite well.

Mr Millgate: I agree. Adding to the previous point, obviously companies always need to be alive to these types of obligations, but there are particular times, where executives within such companies, need to be even more alive to these issues. This may be particularly so when the organisation is going through a low profit period or when there is a lot of new, sensitive information flowing through the company. At those times, these issues need to be approached with an even stricter rigour. Key people in an organisation must be made very well aware of their obligations and much more restrictive approach may be needed in those circumstances than in others. When working within a listed company, you must play your part in maintaining the integrity of the market.

Assoc. Prof. Overland: Matt, would you agree? Does that fit with the types of advice you are often asked to give regarding that intersection?

Mr Egerton-Warburton: Absolutely. The general counsels and the company secretaries often get a lot of pressure from internal people who want to trade. If the company is going well, employees are often thinking they are able to make money from trading. All listed companies have securities trading policies these days but there are always those at the margin which cause companies concern. This may be part of the policy which says that, for a certain period of time after the company has released its annual report, that directors and officers can trade. This is more difficult when the company is in some sort of litigation that the market does not know about, or when there is a transaction brewing which means directors often cannot trade despite the policy seemingly allowing it. We often get phone calls from general counsels asking, 'I'm just not sure whether I should let my directors and officers trade here or not. What do you think?'. So, that is when we get involved. I made a comment to you before that when there are ten enquiries about this internally, we will only hear about the one which is on the margins. This is because the rules are pretty clear now and companies have good internal policies as to what people can and cannot do.

Assoc. Prof. Overland: That is really interesting. Can I also ask, do you think that the use of technology makes your job easier or harder in that respect? Does it have any impact for you?

Mr Millgate: You can receive information very quickly and you can also respond to it very quickly. There are also safeguards you can put against a large employee cohort as well, so that you can restrict trading in a blackout period through the registry. So, there are a few tools at your disposal for that. It is not perfect, but you are certainly able to prioritise high-risk individuals over other parts of an organisation.

Ms Launders: Moreover, when I think of the question about how technology impacts on this issue, for me it is about social media. Particularly, as I work for a media company, we have a large PR team that wants to tell the world about everything that is going on, which is fantastic most of the time, but I do need to be really careful that they understand that there are some things that cannot go out to social media until they have gone to the ASX first. I have a great relationship with our PR team so that all works very smoothly. This eagerness to get the latest exciting news out, can be problematic if it is price sensitive, so we do need to be very aware that the ASX is first on anything which is sensitive. Otherwise, I think that regarding technology, the ease with which information can be spread probably makes it harder to say that something is not generally available. I don't think the ASX is particularly influenced by proliferation of news sources. They are very much focused on 'mainstream media' rather than looking to what online media is speculating about and then doing trading queries to listed companies based on that. So, I think that the ASX is aware of the sources of information, but I think they take a sensible approach to what they query and when, rather than looking at the broad array of blatant news that might be around.

Assoc. Prof. Overland: Matt, do you have a comment on that?

Mr Egerton-Warburton: Yes, I think it is easier to communicate. I think a smart person can work out how to communicate information outside of channels that can be detected. What is very hard to do these days is to trade on that communication because ASIC is very organised. They have very sophisticated systems in place. You might be aware of information that is going to move the market but it is difficult to do anything with it. So, I think that aspect is the tough bit these days. It was easy to do previously but with all the new technology that ASIC has, it is not so easy to do now.

Assoc. Prof. Overland: Yes, thank you. I want to ask you about the NAB scandal. A number of years ago, an employee of NAB was convicted of insider trading and even though that trading had nothing to do with the NAB itself or his role as an employee, there were a number of organisations who became concerned that, if they had a similar experience with a rogue employee who engaged in similar insider trading, they would suffer reputational damage. This is despite the fact that the employees in question may not be employed to trade on behalf of the company. In your experience, in executive management, do you think about these things, not just from a compliance perspective but from a reputational one as well? No-one wants to be the next company whose name is in the news saying, 'Boral employee convicted of insider trading' or 'Channel Nine employee under investigation for insider trading'. Would you have a comment on that perhaps?

Mr Egerton-Warburton: My comment would be that so much of the value of companies these days is based on brand and goodwill. If you take a hit against that, there can be enormous damage not only to your share price but also to other parts of your business. I don't have any concrete advice as to how to deal with rogue employees. You have your policies and you do your best to proliferate information but it is something that companies are too concerned with all day every day because they are trying to protect shareholder value. What is talked about more I think at a broad level, from my experience, is continuous disclosure. Since we have such a class action regime in Australia now, that is very sophisticated, there are people out there who may be waiting to fund the next class action litigation. The easiest way to hit a company now is if they do not continuously disclose information as they should. That, to me, is the big topic around the board table. I don't know if you would both agree with that.

Ms Launders: Yes, absolutely.

Mr Millgate: Absolutely. Just going back to the point you made earlier concerning employees and information that they may pick up regarding other organisations, it is particularly prevalent around joint venture arrangements as sometimes there is a difference in what is sensitive in one organisation versus what is sensitive in another. I think the key thing is to get in front of the people who are involved in these transactions and bring the policies into light. You need to talk about, not only the companies you are dealing with, but about information more generally. It is about you personally. You find these people in the organisation, at these particular times, as these things pop up, and you use that as an opportunity to get out there and educate them about it.

Mr Egerton-Warburton: I have a client at the moment that is planning a significant corporate manoeuvre and they have got a core team in a separate building, with a separate IT system and every document they send out, even to us, is encrypted with a different code. That is one way they are making sure that this policy and plan does not filter down within their organisation. That's particularly sophisticated and it's new but I think we will see more of that going forward.

Assoc. Prof. Overland: There is obviously a significant amount of work that goes into creating such a system, isn't there? It is an exceptional level of security.

Mr Egerton-Warburton: Yes, it is. I'm kind of pleasantly surprised watching this because within a law firm, we are always having to think about ethical walls and 'Chinese Walls' and we do it all day every day but it does not come naturally to a corporate. However, now the big, sophisticated corporates are beginning to think like this as well. For example, when we have a deal in Australia, in a market where there are four or five big law firms, many of the major deals circle around those firms. Often you have a team in Melbourne that is on one side of the deal and a team in Sydney on the other. Or you can have two teams in Sydney on the same side of the deal. We put them on different floors and in different rooms, using different technology systems all the time but it is interesting that corporates are now beginning to do that all internally.

Audience member: Is that a consequence of the particular securities in the transaction? Or is it, as you pointed out earlier, a way that corporates can defend themselves against a class action by arguing that they had done everything that was possible to protect against ill gain? Could there be a number of different factors playing out all at once to enhance governance processes?

Mr Egerton-Warburton: Absolutely. If you can prove, not only to a court but to the public sphere that you did everything reasonable in a situation to protect that information, that goes a long way. Next time you sit in front of a Senate Estimates Committee it will be good to have that track record of what you've done to try and mitigate the risk in that situation.

Audience member: Yes, no guarantee that it will work, but at least you had a go.

Mr Egerton-Warburton: Yes.

Assoc. Prof. Overland: On that note, can I ask you about the use of management time? Thinking of matters going to the level that Matt described, the enormous amount of time spent on these issues comes to mind. The existing insider trading and continuous disclosure obligations require a lot of processes within organisations. Processes to make sure that information is properly filtered, that the people who need to make the disclosure get access to it and that they can do so in a timely way. Overall, there is a significant amount of energy and time that is spent on managing securities trading policies. It seems to be becoming increasingly onerous. Would you be willing to make a comment on the amount of time that you and others spend thinking about these things and how that impacts on your teams and others around you?

Ms Launders: There are a number of things about Channel Nine, my organisation, which make it unique and perhaps explain why our processes are less onerous than for other organisations. We have two parts to our business. On one side of the business, we get content from a wide array of sources but there are really only a couple of key content providers that are material to our business. For example, the NRL and the cricket. There are really no significant changes to those relationships other than every five years or so we re-negotiate them. So when I think about that part of our business, there is not a huge amount that we think is price sensitive but nonetheless we need to manage that. When those sorts of things come up it is a live issue for us. However, there is only a small group of people, at a very senior level, who are involved in such negotiations, so it is very easy for me to make sure that information stays contained and is disclosed at the appropriate time.

On the other side of business, we have revenue largely from advertising and that comes from an enormous array of sources. Once again there is not *one* contract, or one small group of contracts which would be price sensitive. The only thing we would need to be aware of is whether the market is going to have a downturn or an upturn. If that were to happen and our advertising was dropping off, we would need to keep a close eye on that to determine the effect on our revenue and if disclosure would be needed. I have a lot of confidence in our finance team that they are watching that every day and are alert to things which might not be going according to plan. Our CFO and CEO are also on top of that issue every single day, so that is the key things that happen in our business that might cause us issues around that.

Regarding securities trading issues, we've only been listed for around four years and as such we do not have a share plan that is widely spread across the organisation. There is only a very small group of people who would want to be trading our shares and I do not have to spend days of the year looking at requests or having to provide my view. People know of the seven months in the year when they can trade and the five months in the year when they cannot. That prohibited time is generally leading up to accounts and to the AGM. We are very good at communicating to people about what those windows are, when they are open, when they are closed and lots of people are reasonably well trained about when they can trade. If we go into another black out period for some reason, people are told so that they know where they stand. I also think that our staff are not big financial traders, so reputational issues around people insider trading in someone else's shares is not a large concern. I don't think that's a massive issue for my organisation.

Assoc. Prof. Overland: Okay, thank you, what about you Dominic?

Mr Millgate: Yes, we have a fairly similar type of organisation but I think Rachel has certainly already picked out a key point. That is the importance of the finance function of your CFO and of a very close relationship between the CFO, CEO, GC and the IR team in building a working document on market expectations as against your internal projections. This includes knowing your buffer for error. You also get to build your processes so that they are workable. You don't want to create something that is overly onerous.

When you have a larger policy that applies to your whole organisation, sometimes when you are looking at your trading windows and considering when to open, restrict or delay them, you're looking at a much closer view of the business. Looking to your regular communications and active discussions close to trading windows or announcements, it is often only with a core group of the board and the executive team and as such, I don't find it enormously onerous. I feel that in my role that is extremely important. I think there should be an individual, or a series of individuals, alive to the need to each supervise parts of the process. However, you can see some organisations where the policy seems quite onerous.

Assoc. Prof. Overland: Matt, can I turn to you now? You see so many large transactions in the work that you do, whereas a lot of other organisations may have one or two big transactions a year, and then they get to have a bit of a lull. As you are constantly moving from one big transaction to another, what do you see as the biggest challenges in managing the information within those big deals in those three different areas of regulation?

Mr Egerton-Warburton: To answer that question, I'll talk about a deal I did recently which was the world's biggest condom deal, and I'm very proud of that.

Ansell was a listed Australian company and they were selling their condom division for approximately AUD800 million to a Chinese bidder. This is a very common type of transaction in Australia. When they started the process of allowing the bidder to come in and look through their books and look through their company, as this is a listed company, they were hesitant to allow someone to get inside information. This can be a tricky moment. My client, the Chinese bidder, was required to sign a series of documents, including a non-disclosure agreement which required them to have a two-year trading stand still so that they would be able to look at the information of the target company. So for this business, they had to agree on these terms and would be unable to trade for two years. That is a pretty common occurrence and that two-year period was quite long considering that any information which they obtained through the process would probably have become stale within six months or one year. As my client is not a trading company, they said they probably would not have traded shares anyway so they didn't negotiate that too broadly. That's one issue that comes up.

Yes, I think that is about it. Personally, I cannot do anything because I know so much information. We have some lawyers within my firm that want to trade and there's a specific in-house general counsel who deals with them. It is almost impossible because we have anywhere between four and five hundred clients constantly engaging in transactions and your answer must be 'no, you just can't do it'.

Assoc. Prof. Overland: You have to find some particularly obscure little tiny, tiny mining company.

Mr Egerton-Warburton: Exactly. And then the question is why? What do you know?

Assoc. Prof. Overland: I'm going to open questions up to the room now.

Audience member: Thank you very much for the interesting panel discussion. It is certainly very heartening to hear and see the processes and procedures in place around approvals in control of information. My question is perhaps to each of the panellists in relation to the challenges now of hacking and cyber misconduct. Have your respective organisations put your minds to reviewing or increasing vigilance surrounding your systems? I would also like to know whether any of your organisations have been hacked or otherwise and how you might be looking at dealing with that challenge.

Ms Launders: Cyber security is something that gets talked about pretty much every board meeting in some way or another. It is very front of mind. This is partly in response to news every month or so that somebody significant has had a major hack or has been subject to one. Although we have not been subject to such an incident, we are very aware of the possibilities for that, not least because a large part of my business is digitally driven and as such, it is something that we spend a lot of time looking at what we have done and we have increased our resources in that area to protect the organisation.

Mr Millgate: For us, with the mandatory data breach reporting coming up, that is another opportunity to bring that topic to the organisation in a refreshed kind of way. Moreover, in the last nine to 12 months, we have shown desktop data to the board to let them know how many attempts at hacking are flowing through. There are enormous numbers. I think it is about the maturity of your particular IT systems and the security in place to manage that. It is about having a kind of review in place to ensure that the highest point of the organisation, the board, is aware and that you are properly resourced to handle these issues. As these things are changing all of the time, you must make sure regular changes and road maps for improvement are set out alongside a line of sight to the board.

Mr Egerton-Warburton: Well, we had a massive hack the other day, not King & Wood Mallesons but a client that we act for. It is a well-known global offshore fund and would be one of three or four that control enormous amounts of world trade at the moment. They got hacked and 30,000–40,000 documents have been dumped through Wikipedia. I'm not sure how they are being published but that is an enormous worry for us.

I don't quite see it but I know that we've got enormously sophisticated security on all our systems but we had to institute that quite early in the day because we're an Australian law firm that did a merger with a Chinese law firm and one of the first things that happened was that all our biggest domestic clients, including the banks and the big mining houses said, 'We're not going to work with you unless you prove to us that you've got technology in place and that information we give you, here in Australia, doesn't flow through to China'. This puts us in the unusual position of having enormous firewalls between us and our colleagues up in China because everyone is well aware that cyber espionage is a day to day operation in Asia. This is especially so in China where 67 per cent of the economy is state owned enterprise. There are Chinese information security persons who operate hand in hand with the steel company, which obtains information on iron ore prices and at that level I can't think of any other situation around the world where you have that level of sophistication. You would need to be very, very careful and our clients, the BHPs and Rio Tintos, they know all this and so they were very harsh on us when we said we were doing this merger. So, that was quite interesting.

However, I think if someone were to hack my email account and get lots of information, it would be hard for them to trade on it because I might have a deal that is rip roaring today and it'll fall over in two days-time. If they put a position on the market on the anticipation that a take-over is coming, and it falls over the next day, they would need to be a very good hacker but they would also need to have a very sophisticated filter on the information out of a law firm. I really don't know how helpful it would be.

Audience member: Can I get some insight as to your thought processes please? Quite obviously you have got opportunity and engagement processes with people like ASIC because of your need for continuous disclosure, what about the police? Do you actually go straight to police on matters we are speaking about this morning? Or is it usually straight to an external law firm first and then to the police if that decision was made to do that?

Ms Launders: You mean that if we suspected some insider trading or other criminal matters or other issues, from an in-house counsel point of view? It's not something that I've done in the time that I've been in-house at Nine. I know our newsroom deals with the police quite regularly where that is an appropriate course of contact but in relation to securities trading issues, if I had an issue, I would be going to ASIC directly or ASIC would be coming to me as it happened.

Audience member: I suppose my point is that as the law gets more sophisticated the cross over between people like ASIC, the Tax Office and the police, are becoming more involved. Obviously, from a government point of view, people do talk to each other, so no one is in isolation, but there are issues around timing and things like that. That is where my interest stems from.

Ms Launders: Yes, in my securities trading issues if I needed to go to a regulator, I would go to ASIC about that.

Mr Millgate: Yes, I am the same. I have never actually encountered an incident. Police are more involved if you have local theft issues or that kind of thing.

Audience member: What about for a matter concerning international corruption?

Mr Egerton-Warburton: We do get enquiries from in-house counsel saying, 'We've got this problem, how do we deal with it?', but I've never been aware of us going directly to police with that. We would always go to ASIC and we deal with ASIC all day, every day. We have ASIC officers coming to us seeking market intelligence and then we go to them with questions about how to apply a rule. There is actually a very interactive situation.

Assoc. Prof. Overland: Matt, could you also share with us some of your overseas experiences that relate to these issues having worked in Hong Kong and New York? Do those experiences give you a different perspective?

Mr Egerton-Warburton: Yes, in America you have a different system of insider trading that is based upon the ownership of information and fiduciary duties. In America, you cannot insider trade if you do not have a duty to someone about their information. If you were walking down the street in America and a takeover offer flutters down from the sky and you read it, you can go into the New York Stock Exchange and begin trading on that. That would not be an offence, whereas in Australia you could not do that. So there is that difference between the two systems but I think there are other noteworthy differences. We have a clean system in Australia because we have a sophisticated, well-regulated regulator on the beat and the other thing we have in Australia, which you don't have in other jurisdictions, is a sophisticated, vociferous financial media. The Fin Review keeps everyone honest in Australia, whereas in Hong Kong, in Singapore, in Asia because they don't have a very good financial media system, notorious things happen all the time and people just don't know about them. And if they don't know about it, they are not putting pressure on the regulator to do stuff about it. It is a bit of a virtuous cycle we have in Australia. We have a small market but we have a very big, well-resourced paper, that is desperate for content because they have to fill the pages with all their commercial property ads. This reporting then in turn puts pressure on the regulator. We have a pretty clean, well-run system here whereas in other places that is not the case.

Audience member: I think many would be surprised to find that it is insiders within a company, rather than hackers, who play a significant role in these issues. It is a conveniently pleasant thought to think hackers are the threat. However, the threats from inside are just as significant as those from outside.

Assoc. Prof. Overland: And that is certainly what we've seen in the number of cases in the past. It is often the insider who works with the outsider. The outsider does the trading, and the insider passes the information. As that process becomes more sophisticated, the manners of communication become key to tracking such conduct. How sophisticated are the offenders at hiding their communication? Are they blasé and careless and think that they will get away with it? Is there a digital footprint to track or not? Is there metadata to examine afterwards? Are they careful with their trading patterns to win some, lose some? Do they make it look as if they're just having a punt? It becomes very complex.

Audience member: I would be interested to hear the panel's opinion on how important it is to develop a culture which provides whistle-blower processes. Particularly with regards to this insider trading issue that we have been talking about.

Ms Launders: That is imperative. You can have all the policies in the world, you can do all the training that you can possibly squeeze into peoples' days, but if you have for an example, a board that is blasé about compliance within themselves, that is what is setting the tone from the top. I have a Chairman who is the Former Treasurer of Australia and he takes a pretty conservative approach to comply with the Corporations Act, as you would expect. That approach really sets a fantastic tone. Within the media industry, which loves talking about itself, it is important to set a tone that says, 'there is the important obligations and we will comply with them'. For some people in the organisation, it might feel like the most natural thing in the world to talk to journalists before something is ready to be public. Those people know that we need to keep a lid on that kind of activity. So yes, culture from the top is absolutely number one.

Mr Millgate: Yes, I agree. The most delightful thing that can happen is when you have your own employees calling you directly about something which is high risk, or calling you about another individual in their team saying that 'we have this particular information, what do you think?'. It is usually because it's in a small pocket of the organisation and is not really a big issue, but to me a good culture means that employees come to you rather than you needing to constantly push out, restrict or try to do things yourself. That is far less effective.

Mr Egerton-Warburton: As lawyers we can write the most brilliant policies but if there is not a culture to follow them, then they are just useless. We see this all the time in companies that have problems. They have the policies in place, but no one is pushing them to the organisation or adhering to them. That is where culture is so important.

We deal very closely with a group of directors who think it is the key to success and it's something that I think is reasonably new to the Australian corporate culture – that idea of real meaningful compliance in an organisation. It is getting there.

To your other point, we are about to introduce new whistle-blower legislation, as you probably know, which is going to have a significant impact on thinking of these issues in Australia. We are going to replicate the American system. That is a popular discussion at the moment. If you're a whistle-blower, and the company is sued, or the government is sued for $10, 20, 50 million, then you will receive 10 to 15 per cent of that as a bounty system. It has worked pretty well in America. We've never done anything like that in Australia, so it will be interesting to see how we go. I think that will put an enormous amount of pressure on companies. If there is a secretary who knows they can pick up a million bucks if they dob in their boss for bad behaviour ... that will be interesting.

Audience member: Is that in just financial services?

Ms Launders: It's right inside the *Corporations Act* and regarding tax as well. It is also for breach of any Commonwealth law. It is actually much broader than the whistle-blower stuff which is in the *Corporations Act* at the moment. It will be interesting to see how that pans out, even though it is not as large at the US bounty system, there is the potential for some reward.

Assoc. Prof. Overland: This has been a very interesting discussion, with many valuable insights shared. Thank you very much to our panellists and all audience members who participated as well.

Chapter 6

Combatting Financial Crimes in Australia: Some Reflections on What Criminologists Can Contribute

Michael Levi

Criminology is the study of the processes of the making of laws, the breaking of laws and of society's reactions towards the breaking of laws. It normally is the study of 'folk devils':[1] those who are stigmatised in some way and become part of a dynamic of social exclusion. The world of crime demonology used to be so simple. There was the Underworld, consisting of full-time criminals emanating principally from the 'dangerous classes' (whether exported from the UK in the 19th century or not) and, depending on particular conditions, who might form 'organised crime' groups ranging from Mafias such as the 'Ndrangheta' to those popularised in the Australian television series, *Underbelly,* to looser collaborative networks.[2] At the other end of the social spectrum there was the primarily law-abiding Upperworld, whose elite black sheep or rotten apples, barrels or social networks might occasionally stray.[3] Both sets might commit frauds, but, while the Underworld types know that they are committing crimes, the latter might convince themselves that they were not breaking the law, even after the fact.[4] On top of this application of labels to individuals, there is

---

1   Stanley Cohen, *Folk Devils and Moral Panics: The Creation of the Mods and Rockers* (Routledge, 2003).

2   Michael Levi, 'The Organisation of Serious Crimes for Gain', in Mike Maguire, Rod Morgan and Robert Reiner (eds.), *The Oxford Handbook of Criminology* (Oxford University Press, 2012) 595.

3   David Enrich, *The Spider Network* (HarperCollins, 2017).

4   Michael L. Benson and Sally S. Simpson, *White-Collar Crime: An Opportunity Perspective* (Routledge, 2015); Michael Levi. *Theoretical Perspectives on White-Collar Crime* (forthcoming) Oxford Research Encyclopedia Online; Eugene Soltes. *Why*

the potential (or lack of it) for demonisation of corporations, memorialised brilliantly in the title 'No soul to damn – no body to kick – an unscandalised inquiry into the problem of corporate punishment'.[5]

Sutherland sought to connect these separate worlds of crime by his stress on criminality as learned behaviour and the argument that white-collar crime *was* organised crime (but *not capitalised* Mafia-style 'Organised Crime').[6] He did not, however, truly consider the depth of rationalisations by elites or the legal and moral difficulties caused for executive culpability when subordinates simply do not follow criminal instructions but rather second-guess what would please their superiors and advance their own careers (if undetected or even if detected). Corporate culpability is a social and legal construction which varies hugely between countries (a fact that needs to be taken into account when evaluating prosecutorial 'success' cross-border). In recent years, Volkswagen and its corporate associates (and perhaps others) engaged in globally massive, deliberate, falsification of toxic diesel emission levels to achieve enhanced corporate sales targets and profits;[7] we readers should consider why this is not commonly labelled as 'organised crime' or even 'white-collar crime' unless criminal prosecution occurs?[8] It is speculative to consider what might have been the impact on criminology and crime control had Sutherland in the 1940s publicly named the US corporations whose 'criminal careers' he analysed, using techniques that were very basic when compared with today's WikiLeaks-fuelled investigations by the International Consortium of Investigative Journalists.

They Do It: Inside the Mind of the White-Collar Criminal (Public Affairs, 2016).

5   John C. Coffee, 'No Soul to Damn – No Body to Kick – An Unscandalised Inquiry into the Problem of Corporate Punishment' (1981) 79(3) *Michigan Law Review* 386.

6   Edwin H. Sutherland, *White-Collar Crime: The Uncut Version* (Yale University Press, first published 1939, 1983 edn.).

7   Jack Ewing, *Faster, Higher, Farther: The Inside Story of the Volkswagen Scandal* (WH Norton, 2017).

8   In addition, car industry political lobbyists successfully (and legally) got EC officials to sustain the inappropriate method of lab-based testing to make their European emissions and pollution levels look better than they merited in real world tests.

The tensions involved in deciding whether to use criminal law or regulatory mechanisms to control some or all 'market misconduct' are not unique, but the power to license firms and individuals has few parallels in the ordinary world or even the world outside financial services (at least where there are not trade sanctions in place). We may all have different views about what 'effectiveness' constitutes: does it require putting executives in jail as a symbolic gesture of fairness, or are we to work out a more cerebral form of 'crime reduction' or 'harm reduction' in which the routine symbolism and retributivism of the criminal process is subordinated – indeed eclipsed altogether? How important is rapid compensation in determining the model of what action is taken, and how important *should* it be?

In the post-truth era, it is, and should be, proper to concern ourselves with the legitimacy of the financial sector and how it should be analysed, justified and controlled. This includes the role of regulators and of criminal prosecution in holding commerce to account, as well as in preventing detriment to commerce by both insiders and outsiders (such as by loosely construed 'organised crime'). It is important to understand that, like 'law and order', regulator-regulated relationships, and the denotation of what conduct is regulated, comprise a dynamic which can shift with the political environment and is influenced by scandal. Nonetheless, how far domestic or international scandal disrupts the tectonic plates of national and globalised economies is an open empirical question.

The work of Tom Tyler and his adherents on why most people obey the law[9] argues that social legitimacy of law is obtained to a large measure by procedural justice, and that this model shifts our thinking in the direction of how the policed 'communities' see what is happening to them rather than our taking controllers' perspectives as proxies for those of 'society'. Criminologists mostly study this in the context of issues such as stopping and searching, or surveillance, of minorities, violent police-citizen or denizen encounters, 'crimmigration', etc. In many parts of the world, the increase in

---

9   Though self-reported delinquency studies reveal otherwise. It would be more accurate to state that most people obey most laws most of the time.

'hate crimes' stimulated by majoritarian nationalistic movements and their politicians raises important questions about what we mean by legitimacy and whose take on legitimacy we are interested in.[10] This legitimacy issue can be, but seldom has been, applied to white-collar crimes of different types.[11] Tyler himself focuses on reducing employee crime via enhanced fairness and perceived fairness of procedures. However, some neglected problems arise in this perspective about the importance of listening to 'policed communities', a notion developed in the context of listening to relatively powerless ones. For example, when companies believe that they are being 'over-regulated' in relation to harmful externalities generated by their businesses, we would not automatically abandon attempts to regulate them. But in a 'light touch regulation' era – whether this light touch is an explicit political or bureaucratic goal, or merely happens implicitly by resource starvation – this pushback from powerful sectors of the political economy influences the climate of control. Thus, even those cases we do know about, because of the lapse of time from the date of offending (which can occur over many years or at a brief point in time) until its coming to light and being the subject of court action, find themselves subject to criticisms for things done, or often not done, in a different political climate. Many regulation and restorative justice scholars, however, argue that regulation is more effective if businesses were at least partly 'onside'. Legitimacy in the eyes of businesspeople would be considered ideally desirable,[12] even though it may require a continuity and strength of purpose that are hard to maintain politically over time.

---

10 Collective Bargaining by Riot is one way of getting elites interested in improving resources for lower social and ethnic groups, though they have other consequences, including savage repression in some contexts.

11 See Michael Levi, 'Legitimacy, Crimes and Compliance in "the City": *De Maximis non Curat Lex?*' in Justice Tankebe and Alison Liebling (eds.), *Legitimacy and Criminal Justice: An International Exploration* (Oxford University Press, 2013) 157; Tom R. Tyler, 'Reducing Corporate Criminality: The Role of Values' (2014) 51(1) *American Criminal Law Review* 267.

12 Peter Drahos (ed.), *Regulatory Theory: Foundations and Applications* (ANU Press, 2017).

The extent to which it is likely that business and a 'sufficient' number of staff[13] are, in fact, 'onside' may depend on the type of misconduct and market conditions. This may require both external pressure and internal monitoring. In the particular case of the mis-selling of Payment Protection Insurance in the UK, this serious and endemic misconduct accounted for a significant proportion of some bank profits, and without some risk of prosecution or condign regulatory penalty, it might have been difficult to stop. Labelling it as mis-selling rather than (arguably) as fraud almost certainly assisted the substantial reparation, which to date has cost the banks some £34 billion, including legal and administrative costs. But it is unknown whether exposure alone would have led to the *rapid* abandonment of the practice. After all, there is little evidence that advertising harms or changes behaviour quickly (though the UK Financial Conduct Authority's recent heavy advertising of the ending of PPI claims via 'RoboCop'-type adverts appears to have generated a significant increase in claims).[14]

It is important to be clear about the research questions we are seeking to address, including, from a criminological perspective, the following:

1. Does the behaviour of elites, their policing and accountability to justice (broadly construed) have some demonstration effect on the propensity of others to commit street and household crime, be that effect either negative or positive?

2. Does inaction (or perceived inaction) against elites make

---

13 This can vary by the type of business. In many of the international financial services scandals, it is moot how many people of which status within particular lines of business can cause substantial harm.

14 For an examination of this, see Financial Conduct Authority, *FCA PPI Campaign* (2019) <https://www.fca.org.uk/ppi/>; Financial Conduct Authority, *PPI Campaign Response Update* (13 December 2018) <https://www.fca.org.uk/news/news-stories/ppi-campaign-response-update>. For a criticism of the response of the Financial Ombudsman Service, see James Salmon and Claudia Joseph, 'Up to Half a Million Victims of the PPI Mis-selling Scandal Were 'Cheated out of Compensation by the Financial Ombudsman', *Daily Mail* (online), 12 March 2018 <https://www.dailymail.co.uk/news/article-5489067/Up-500-000-victims-cheated-PPI-compensation.html>.

the public, and non-elite offenders, think that crime-control policy and/or society generally is unfair (and if so, so why)?

3. Of greatest direct interest to regulators and their statutory remit, what is the impact of regulatory and criminal justice actions on levels of misconduct or particular types of financial crime? This can be most fruitfully broken down into different forms of consumer detriment, but may also have some effect on the dynamism of economies.

Of these questions, regulators usually concern themselves explicitly only with the third question and they may not consider the impact of prosecutions that may be outside their control. Indeed, each individual regulator may not find it worthwhile to look at issues they are not organisationally set up to handle, a point that can be observed in the responses in the closing stages of the interim phase of the Royal Commission into Misconduct in the Banking, Superannuation and Financial Services Industry (November 2018) ('Royal Commission'). The evidence, however, presented to the Commission and media reactions thereto suggest that the exposure has struck a chord about:

1. The scale of financial crimes and misconduct among most major Australian financial institutions (in a narrower range than occurred in the UK and US);

2. The failures of the regulators and criminal justice agencies to spot, and act, against the firms and/or their 'rogue individuals' (as asserted by the CEO of AMP November 2018, to some scepticism!); and

3. The gaps in role and approach between different regulators and criminal justice bodies.

For criminologists, much depends on what one means by 'white-collar crime', a term which stretches from blue-collar crime to elite malfeasance, with 'organised fraud' being ambiguously located in white-collar and/or in organised crime.[15] Tyler's analysis of legitimacy and adherence to rules by employees is interesting and empirically grounded. Also, the flurry of Australian, and international, criminal and regulatory cases since 2012 that cover a range of bank misconduct occurring over several years – in relation to money laundering, fraud, insider dealing, rogue trading and sanctions evasion – have reinforced the challenge and importance of corporate discipline. A different perspective would be that, given a low objective, and perceived, likelihood or severity of sanctions, or even publicity, at the time, corporate leaders had little disincentive to allow or encourage law-breaking of this kind. A theorist might ask why they would be likely to motivate conformity with law, rather than maximise corporate or business unit profits from which they benefited personally by bonuses, continued employment or global marketability. To the extent that the individuals considered risks or morality at all in addition to views about likely penalties, their estimates of time between offending, exposure or formal action would be expected to be central – celerity is an issue which is more salient in corporate misconduct than elsewhere – given the concealment potential in many such crimes – unless management is proactively trying to reduce them.

But it would be hard to dispute that the more significant problem of legitimacy is the, at best, partial adherence of global elites to legal rules that are nowadays near-universal (like criminal and regulatory rules against money laundering, financing terrorism and Grand Corruption) or that are sometimes patchy and country-specific (like conflict of interest rules, and the criminalisation of price-fixing cartels or insider trading).[16] The effects of this 'extra-legal behaviour' by elites on the behaviour of their employees and other citizens – be they persistent offenders, occasional offenders or even the rather small subset of people who have never offended at all –

---

15 Levi, above n 4.

16 Though there has been a global trend towards criminalisation in these spheres, the forms of international pressure generated by the FATF are not as present there.

remain largely to be analysed. It is one thing to show that, before and/or after their involvement in crimes, street criminals and 'the Underworld' use techniques of neutralisation,[17] it is another to argue that the relative impunity of elites increases the harm and frequency of those other crimes. Nor is it at all clear what the level of actual or – arguably more important – *perceived* elite crime would have to be to reduce these moral and morale effects on the rest of the vulnerable population.

There are many examples in which financial services sales employees are encouraged to disobey (or, to be more generous, are deliberately not discouraged from disobeying) the law.[18] Mortgage broking deceptions of sub-prime borrowers in the US are a less clear-cut case versus the mis-selling of Personal Protection Insurance in the UK, for many of these occurred in amoral small investment firms and some hyper-aggressive larger firms, though these tactics were later adopted by an industry leader, Countrywide Assurance, when it was undercut and found it impossible to get business;[19] a process which repeated itself in the property business in Ireland after Anglo-Irish Bank began to scoop all the chances to make money (*sic*) from property developers as a result of its easy loan business model. The short-run profits this generated contributed significantly to the personal benefits received by the directors, the valuations of the companies and the apparent prosperity of the economies in which the firms were based. Through derivatives sales to global banks, these vast losses that were, at best, very negligently spread to other countries.

---

17 Techniques of neutralisation involve judging what they see as the harms of their own crimes against a suite of crimes to diminish their own misconduct in their own eyes and of those they identify with and care about: Shadd Maruna and Heith Copes, 'Excuses, Excuses: What Have We Learned from Five Decades of Neutralisation Research?' in Michael Tonry (ed.), *Crime and Justice* (Chicago University Press, 2004).

18 One example is the Personal Protection Insurance 'mis-selling' – which was arguably systemic fraud – in the UK that occurred for a decade after 2001, and which was met with immense reluctance by the banks to compensate their customers: Financial Ombudsman Service, 'Annual Review: 2011–12' (Report, Financial Ombudsman Service, 2012); Financial Ombudsman Service, 'Annual Review: 2017–18' (Report, Financial Ombudsman Service, 2018).

19 Bethany McLean and Joe Nocera, *All the Devils Are Here: Unmasking the Men Who Bankrupted the World* (Viking, 2011).

Early white-collar crime literature focused on the ways in which senior directors and employees alike were sucked into crimes 'for the firm' by differential association models in which they learned to do what was *profitable* over what was moral.[20] Later on, embezzlement against the firm's interests was explained away as not real crime but rather as 'just borrowing'.[21] This capacity for seeing oneself as essentially good (or, at least, as complying with the norms of one's peers and, 'therefore', not being culpable) is a common theme in Australian and other banking misconduct. Also central to explanations about bank misconduct are perverse financial incentives in that, even where bankers believe or suspect their conduct is morally, ethically or even perhaps legally wrong, the desire to obtain bonuses (and *bigger* bonuses) clouds their decision-making. This has even greater effect when there is groupthink about bonuses. The problem is unlikely to go away because bankers are highly resistant and have been largely successful in stopping regulators from intervening in their system of remuneration. In Australia, since 2011, there has been a two strikes rule, which means that the entire company board can face re-election if shareholders on two occasions object to the remuneration package put before a general meeting. It is an open question whether the two strikes rule has affected the accountability of directors.[22] As concerns managers below director level, little has changed with regard to the bonus system. Interestingly, after the money laundering scandal involving the Commonwealth Bank, the board agreed to cut the short-term bonus of the CEO, and it was reported that about 400 executives of CBA have lost more than $100 million in bonuses.[23] Whether this example, or the fallout from the Royal Commission, has any wider and longer-term effect on bonuses remains to be seen.

Tyler distinguishes between 'compliance with the law and voluntary, willing acceptance of the law', the latter being particularly salient 'in work

---

20 Sutherland, above n 6.

21 Donald Cressey, *Other People's Money* (Free Press, 1953).

22 See MinterEllison, *Research on Australia's 'Two Strikes' Rule* (22 August 2016) <https://www.minterellison.com/articles/research-on-australias-two-strikes-rule>.

23 Commonwealth Bank of Australia, 'Annual Report: 2018' (Report, Commonwealth Bank of Australia, 2018).

settings' since it predicts rule-following even where there is no perceived risk of detection.[24] Of course, he (and other authors)[25] are correct in flagging the limitations of deterrence and cruder forms of rational choice theory in accounting for why people obey the law. Competing accounts for banker misconduct range from largely genetic sociopathy that can be more easily 'activated' in rip-off cultures[26] via 'irrational exuberance',[27] 'animal spirits'[28] and poor decision-making heuristics,[29] affected by factors including excessive concentrations of testosterone in dealing rooms,[30] and corrupt cultures that transmit how to be corrupt and how to feel comfortable with that, etc. Where does or *might* legitimacy feature in this behavioural economics of elites? Can we deduce it independently of their behaviour, and, given the opacity of the conduct of individuals – except via civil lawsuits, Unexplained Wealth Orders, and sometimes criminal prosecutions or Deferred Prosecution Agreements – how are we to be able to infer their individual contributions to those bad outcomes that we do come to learn about?[31]

Global banks and other corporations are vulnerable to misconduct allegations in one part of the globe casting their integrity and/or competence in a negative light, thus potentially undermining the millions they spend on creating a positive corporate image. This is a good potential lever, but

24 Tom R. Tyler, 'Self-Regulatory Approaches to White-Collar Crime: The Importance of Legitimacy and Procedural Justice' in Sally S. Simpson and David Weisburd (eds.), *The Criminology of White-Collar Crime* (Springer, 2009) 195, 199.

25 See Sally S. Simpson, *Corporate Crime, Law, and Social Control* (Cambridge University Press, 2002).

26 Paul Babiak and Robert D. Hare, *Snakes in Suits: When Psychopaths Go to Work* (HarperCollins, 2007).

27 Robert J. Shiller, *Irrational Exuberance* (Princeton University Press, 3rd rev. edn., 2016).

28 George A. Akerlof and Robert J. Shiller, *Animal Spirits: How Human Psychology Drives the Economy, and Why It Matters for Global Capitalism* (Princeton University Press, 2010).

29 Daniel Kahneman, *Thinking, Fast and Slow* (Allen Lane, 2011).

30 John H. Coates, *The Hour Between Dog and Wolf: Risk-taking, Gut Feelings and the Biology of Boom and Bust* (Fourth Estate, 2012).

31 William S. Laufer, *Corporate Bodies and Guilty Minds: The Failure of Corporate Criminal Liability* (University of Chicago Press, 2006).

how do we know what its effects are or what happens when most or all of the financial institutions are revealed to be behaving badly (or to have behaved badly in the recent past)?

I. Regulatory Approaches and Legitimacy

There has been an episodic shift in regulatory theories between countries and over time, none of which are obviously more effective than any other.[32] In the UK, principles-based regulation ('PBR'), heavily promoted by the regulators and the UK government just before the financial crisis, became instantly outmoded. Hector Sants – then chief executive of the Financial Services Authority[33] – pithily observed that a 'principles-based approach does not work with people who have no principles'.[34] The FSA – alongside other UK regulators – moved to 'outcomes-focused' regulation, though the difference between the two is arguably more apparent than real.[35] The US Securities and Exchange Commission ('SEC'), for example, which regulates mainly through prescriptive and detailed rules, and with an aggressive approach to enforcement, notoriously failed to detect the Madoff fraud, sixteen years after the first warning signs appeared.[36] Australia has been on an analogous journey with ASIC and other regulators. In regard to regulatory theory, there is a tendency to take a binary position – principles based v rules based – whereas the position in practice is far more complex. The fact is, the banking system before the Global Financial Crisis was subject to detailed prescriptive rules in many areas, but not in the areas

---

32 Julia Black, 'Paradoxes and Failures: "New Governance" Techniques and the Financial Crisis' (2012) 75(6) *Modern Law Review* 1037.

33 Sants later became head of compliance, and government and regulatory relations, at Barclays after their large regulatory fines in 2012, before resigning exhausted in 2013 and returning to the sector sometime later as a consultant.

34 Hector Sants, 'Delivering Intensive Supervision and Credible Deterrence' (Speech delivered at the Reuters Newsmakers event, London, 12 March 2009).

35 Ibid.

36 Office of Investigations, Securities and Exchange Commission, 'Investigation of Failure of the SEC to Uncover Bernard Madoff's Ponzi Scheme – Public Version –' (Report No OIG-509, Office of Investigations, Securities and Exchange Commission, 31 August 2009) 41.

which gave rise to the systemic issues, such as wholesale derivatives trading. This was based partly on the belief that it could be left to the market to regulate wholesale actors, a belief which was shattered by the GFC. It is moot whether the GFC would have been prevented had the rules been in place but not monitored or enforced intensively. If we are not careful, these debates can descend into tautology.

Another problem with regulatory theories is that they do not inform regulators as to what areas should be the primary focus of enforcement. The US SEC is a good example of this. The SEC has earned its aggressive reputation because of its focus and relative success in insider trading prosecutions. Insider trading is arguably corrupt but seldom directly harmful to counter-parties, and it is not known what the general public think of such behaviour and how they would prioritise it among competing policing resources. Ponzi frauds such as Madoff never received attention by the SEC, even though Ponzi frauds are far more harmful than insider trading. Why has the SEC not been more seriously damaged in regard to its condign failure to stop Madoff, probably the biggest fraud in the 20th century? One factor is that the SEC propagandisation of its successes in insider trading has provided a narrative which preserves its public reputation. Another example is that, after the GFC, Irish regulators admitted that they had missed the signs of systemic risk in the property market (and its financing) because they were focusing on compliance with Basel 2 – watching the wrong ball. In Australia, the tendency to load up bodies such as ASIC with enhanced responsibilities *without* extra resources is obvious. This tendency has also been present in Australian and UK law enforcement for economic crimes, and in international agencies such as Europol and Interpol, given that these agencies have had to adapt to a rising tide of financial crimes – from high-volume cyber-enabled, to low-volume, high-difficulty, transnational fraud, without corresponding increases in their budgets.

Though little serious thought has been given to what constitutes the optimal prosecution rate (for what purposes?), it is commonplace to try to account for the relatively low prosecution and censure rate by regulators and prosecutors in terms of regulatory 'capture culture', as used in financial and industrial regulation. Given the cultural and ideological power of free market economics, however, an alternative view might be to attribute it as much to rapture as to capture;[37] though the revolving door of public-private interchange offers economic as well as intellectual incentives to be moderate in criticism of commercial practices when one may be later seeking employment in the private sector. It is not currently known how much legitimacy the regulators enjoy or what that constitutes, given that institutional evaluations are somewhat bland and that commentators may not be confident about their anonymity. Therefore, perspectives are refracted through representatives of different bodies and experts, at least until events such as the Royal Commission lift the lid on the (lack of) competence and energy with which regulators have acted.

III. Criminal Sanctioning and Legitimacy

In March 1985, a Gallup Poll created by this author found that 50 per cent of the British public (compared with 35 per cent in 1969) believe that the courts favour the rich and influential. This popular judgement may be unfair, inasmuch as – at least at that time and even in the current era – so few rich and influential persons have been prosecuted in the past that the Australian and British courts have had little opportunity to discriminate in favour of them (or not). Legitimacy judgements also impact on trial outcomes, at least in societies in which juries decide on criminal guilt. Most of the discussion of jury decision-making in white-collar crimes has focused on its analytical competence (or otherwise) for dealing with difficult issues,[38] but there are also legitimacy-related questions of how verdicts are affected by public beliefs about whether or not:

---

37 Nicholas Dorn, 'The Governance of Securities: Ponzi Finance, Regulatory Convergence, Credit Crunch' (2010) 50(1) *British Journal of Criminology* 23; Nicholas Dorn, *Democracy and Diversity in Financial Market Regulation* (Routledge, 2014).

38 Michael Levi, 'Blaming the Jury: Frauds on Trial' (1983) 10(2) *Journal of Law and Society,* 257; Michael Levi, 'The Role of the Jury in Complex Cases' in Mark Findlay and Peter Duff (eds.) *The Jury Under Attack* (Butterworths, 1988).

1. the law is justified;
2. the prosecutors and their witnesses have integrity; and
3. the defendant has been unjustifiably singled out for prosecution and is any worse morally than those who are giving evidence for the prosecution.

Acquittals under these circumstances are sometimes referred to as 'jury equity verdicts'.[39] The separable issue of verdict legitimacy in the eyes of defendants might also be important to some and may affect recidivism, though there is no evidence of this.

Jury convictions may add legitimacy compared with judge-alone verdicts, unless jurors are successfully depicted as corrupt or populist dupes of the prosecution. It is unknown whether professionals or 'Masters of the Universe' would find the judgement of fellow professionals to be legitimate. They might take the view that professionals were trying to eliminate competitors or were acting on behalf of elite interests in showing that something was being done. Conversely, the public might see acquittals by professionals as elites 'looking after their own'. All of these are hypothetical in the absence of research on verdict legitimacy in cases such as those sent to Australian courts.[40]

A particularly serious problem facing courts in the UK and Australia, which affects the concept of legitimacy is the challenge of ensuring a fair trial, is ensuring that the jury are not affected by extraneous matters in their decision as to whether a person is guilty of a crime. The general public may not accept this so-called elitist or protective view of a fair trial. Questions the public may consider are:

---

39 Even where there is no jury trial, public perceptions of the questions posed earlier can be important to how the judgements are received, including public protests.

40 For broader discussions of jury legitimacy and nullification issues, see Valerie P. Hans, 'What Difference Does a Jury Make?' (2012) 3(1) *Yonsei Law Journal* 36, 50–3; Paula Hannaford-Agor and Valerie P. Hans, 'Nullification at Work? A Glimpse from the National Center for State Courts Study of Hung Juries' (2003) 78 *Chicago-Kent Law Review* 1249.

1. Why should a jury not have all information before it (for example, evidence of previous convictions); and

2. Why should the jury not view social media commentary during their deliberations?

One of the unfortunate and presumably unintended consequences of orders suppressing publication of connected cases is that the general public are not informed about verdicts in a timely manner. That may affect their denunciatory impact. For example, we learnt in 2018 that Securency and Note Printing Australia pled guilty in 2012 to conspiracy to bribe foreign political leaders and were fined A\$21.6 million. This revelation was a side note to the High Court decision upholding the trial judge's decision that the criminal prosecution of the CEO, CFO, and other individuals allegedly responsible for arranging the bribes, should be stayed on the grounds of abuse of process.[41]

Perhaps this 'simpler age' construction also applies to executives' views of the severity of different penalties. Levi argued that the data in Table 5 from a survey designed by this author showed the susceptibility of those elites embedded in respectability to social and penal sanctions.[42] Professional exclusion was viewed more seriously than two years in an open prison (the most likely real-world result at the time) and even prosecution without conviction was highly salient. Unfortunately, this study has not been replicated, so we cannot tell whether or not the findings would differ today.[43] Furthermore, they are unlikely to apply to the probably thicker-

---

41 See Strickland (a Pseudonym) v DPP (Cth) (2018) 361 ALR 23; and for a commentary, see Jonathan J. Rusch, Australian Foreign-Bribery Investigation of Banknote Firms Nears End on Discordant and Surprising Notes (29 November 2018) Dipping Through Geometries <https://dippingthroughgeometries. blog/2018/11/29/australian-foreign-bribery-investigation-of-banknote-firms-nears-end-on-discordant-and-surprising-notes/>.

42 Michael Levi, 'Suite Justice or Sweet Charity? Some Explorations of Shaming and Incapacitating Business Fraudsters' (2002) 4(2) *Punishment and Society* 147.

43 See George Gilligan et al, 'Penalties Regimes to Counter Corporate and Financial Wrongdoing in Australia – Views of Governance Professionals' (2017) 11(1) *Law and Financial Markets Review* 4 for the views of Australian governance professionals.

skinned career fraudsters, and corporate raiders or global elites.[44]

Table 5. UK Executive Perceptions
of the Relative Severity of Alternative Sanctions

Sentence/Sanction	Severity 0–20
5 years' imprisonment	16.3
2 years' imprisonment in an 'ordinary' closed prison	11.5
Being banned from one's profession for life	10.8
2 years' imprisonment in an open prison	9.3
Publicity for one's offending in national press and tv	9.0
Being shunned by former friends and colleagues	7.9
Dismissal from current job	7.8
2 years' probation plus weekend imprisonment	7.3
Being prosecuted by the SFO, but acquitted by the jury	6.5
Being banned from company directorship for 10 years	5.9
£100,000 fine	5.8
240 hours community punishment	3.3
2 years' probation	2.9

The author's intermittent interviews with American, and other knowledgeable, public officials (2001–17) suggest that the decline in prosecutions was attributable mainly to the shift in focus of federal authorities to counter-terrorism work after the 9/11 attacks, though there was a brief slurry of investigative activity post-Enron to deal with that collapse and the 'dot.com' bubble, and with corporate elites who flagrantly treated corporate assets as personal ones. Hagan attributes regulatory quiescence to the enduring influence of 'the Age of Reagan' which replaced

---

44 Michael Levi, 'Serious Tax Fraud and Non-Compliance: A Review of Evidence
    on the Differential Impact of Criminal and Non-Criminal Proceedings' (2010)
    9(3) *Criminology and Public Policy* 493.

the 'Age of Roosevelt'; Morgenson and Rosner to the 'revolving door' between Wall Street, Congress and the Executive.[45] Whatever the causes – stimulated by the need to raise vast sums for electoral success in the US and the American appellate courts' narrowing of the legal framework for fraud and corruption during the present decade – there are, in essence, fewer pressures to seek out criminal sanctions for elites, whereas there is mainly a fiscal bar on prosecuting and imprisoning those who can be constructed as 'the undeserving poor'.

The legitimacy literature underestimates the difficulty of prosecuting certain types of white-collar crime (e.g. foreign bribery where the evidence is overseas, especially in uncooperative countries) and the ethical constraints for doing so in countries such as Australia. It is not just a question of resources, but also that methods of investigation and prosecution that are regarded as legal (and legitimate) in some countries (e.g. the US) are regarded as illegal, illegitimate or unethical in other countries. This includes sting operations, the 'overcharging' of defendants and methods of turning of suspects into prosecution witnesses via the prospect of greatly reduced sentences for cooperation with the prosecutor. The problem is compounded when regulators and prosecutors are risk averse, as has often been the position in Australia. Unless there is a change in the regulatory and prosecution culture, it is difficult to see how there will be more successful criminal enforcement of a scale or significance which will affect public perceptions. Nor is it clear whether public perceptions are improved or concerns enhanced, rather than reduced, by prosecutions that reveal previously unsuspected misconduct. This applies to corruption and money laundering, and is a global issue. One may query, for example, the impact of the Danske Bank scandal in 2018 on Denmark's and Estonia's Transparency International Corruption Perceptions Index ranking in the future, though the misconduct revealed took place over years when they were ranked as very clean (and the alleged predicate crimes occurred principally in Russia).

---

45 John Hagan, *Who Are the Criminals? The Politics of Crime Policy from the Age of Roosevelt to the Age of Reagan* (Princeton University Press, 2012); Gretchen Morgenson and Joshua Rosner, *Reckless Endangerment: How Outsized Ambition, Greed, and Corruption Led to Economic Armageddon* (Times/Henry Holt, 2011).

IV. Bank Scandals and Their Implications

The era since the Global Financial Crisis has seen a flurry of activity against banks by regulators and prosecutors who were previously 'let off the leash' by 'light touch' regulation. Considering criminal and regulatory cases together, many major banks have been sanctioned in the UK or, more often, in the US, but barely at all in other financial services centres such as Australia.[46] Within the financial crime category from 2013 to 2017, the top five areas relate to sanctions breaches (US$10.1 billion), followed by bribery (US$5.6 billion), tax evasion (US$5.1 billion), fraud (US$4.4 billion) and AML breaches (US$3.5 billion). In this period, the Duff & Phelps data show that Australian fines totalled a third of those in Hong Kong, 3.8 per cent of those in the UK and 0.126 per cent of US regulatory penalties.[47] Rather than engage in an equalisation of penalties, however, we might do better to ask what is the appropriate ratio of fines to misconduct levels, especially given that both misconduct levels vary and *prevention*, not penalisation, is a core object of regulation? The potential effects of the publicity given in these cases on public views of bankers' integrity or their sense of 'fair justice' is hard to articulate or demonstrate. In principle, one might think of legitimacy aims in two contexts:

1. Getting financial institutions and professionals to behave better even when they expect *not* to be punished for behaving badly (as well as when they do think there is a risk of punishment); and
2. Satisfying the public (or at least segments thereof) that the 'Rich and Powerful' are not being treated in an unduly favourable way.

Australian data on some aspects of public perspectives have begun to appear. Even in late 2016, before the main work of the Royal Commission,

---

46 See, for example, Duff & Phelps, 'Global Enforcement Review: Exploring the Impact of Regulatory Enforcement on the Global Financial Services Industry' (Report, Duff & Phelps, 2018).

47 Ibid.

Australian data showed that trust in banks and insurance companies was significantly lower than the global average, and Australians said they were more likely to trust an *employee* of an organisation than its chief executive.[48] A representative national survey in August 2018 showed that, although people tend to trust their own bank more than banks in general, just under a third of the Australian public believe that regulators are doing a good job in holding banks to account, while only 20 per cent think that banks in general are ethical.[49]

A series of major non-American banks – HSBC, Credit Suisse, BNP Paribas, Standard Chartered, Lloyds TSB, ING Bank and ABN AMRO – have been prosecuted or fined by US regulators for stripping the identifiers from transactions in relation to countries like Iran that are subject to *US* (and, in some cases, UN) sanctions, an ongoing source of tension between *Europe* and the US over Iran today. There, the motivation is also profit, but interviews with convenience-sampled compliance officers suggest that the sanctions are, or were, at the time, seen as illegitimate by a significant number of *European* bankers. Whether the *American* bankers saw the controls as legitimate and refrained from violations for that reason, or whether they were just aware that *their* government would act vigorously against them (i.e. there was a credible threat that worked on those issues, and/or their management exerted more surveillance) is unknown. The longevity of institutional awareness is also a significant issue in sustaining reform: in the aftermath of scandal, large sums are spent on compliance, but how long the scrutiny lasts is an open question.

Despite the creation of a seemingly impressive set of AML controls at these big banks, many of them seemed comfortable with continued violations of *their own* rules. The reputational cost, at least as expressed in share prices, is minimal, possibly because banks are already little esteemed, but also because the 'nuclear option' of prosecuting banks or taking away

---

48 Edelman, '2018 Edelman Trust Barometer: Financial Services Edition' (Report, Edelman, 2018).

49 Deloitte, *The Way Forward to Rebuild Reputation and Trust: Deloitte Trust Index – Banking 2018* (29 October 2018) <https://www2.deloitte.com/au/en/pages/media-releases/articles/the-way-forward-rebuild-reputation-trust-291018.html>.

their licenses has been reserved for marginal players: the collateral damage of drastic action being deemed too high (as the bankers doubtless know). It is well-known from deterrence research that expected sanction celerity and certainty are more important than severity.[50] Although this general model of deterrence has not been tested on corporations, elite individuals or 'organised crime'[51] groups, it seems plausible that it is applicable here too.

A key challenge for behavioural change is how to transmit credible signals that get enough attention at senior operational levels in the hierarchy of these corporates, though enhancing legitimacy is only part of that process: deterrence and transparency are also salient. At the bank level, 'too big to be prosecuted' typically leads to tough conditions as an alternative to prosecution and probable internal reform in corporations (arguably a good thing); but it also undermines equality of treatment and perhaps legitimacy when small banks (e.g. in Mexico) get prosecuted and big banks (e.g. American, Australian and British ones) get Deferred Prosecution Agreements or a regulatory fine. Neither proportionality nor individual culpability operate in the same way as they do for 'normal' crimes for gain. There is no sign that cross-crime type consistency is a serious concern. Prima facie, one might have expected tax fraud and social security fraud to be scaled along the same dimensions, given that they are both offences against the government and taxpayers. But the discourse of 'welfare scroungers' remains a dominant leitmotif which has not yet been translated into the media and political discourse about bank misconduct.

Levi has falsified the common view that frauds by elites and by others are neglected in tabloid and broadsheet media.[52] Although this has not been updated to take account of recent scandals, inspection of headlines shows

---

50 Daniel S. Nagin, 'Deterrence in the Twenty-First Century: A Review of the Evidence' in Michael Tonry (ed.) *Crime and Justice: A Review of the Research* (University of Chicago Press, 2013) vol. 42, 199.

51 This term is reasonably applicable to some Australian and global corporates who have committed sustained violations for profit, even though they are only 'part-time offenders'.

52 Michael Levi, 'The Media Construction of Financial White-Collar Crimes' (2006) 46 *British Journal of Criminology* 1037.

that large fines on household-name banks attract publicity in all news media, though significantly more in business papers such as the *Financial Times*, *New York Times*, *Wall Street Journal* and *Australian Financial Review*, that are interested even when the institutions are not household names. Though there are national variations, messages are mixed not (or not just) because of favouritism but because of:

1. relatively low staffing resources compared with the high investigative and prosecution costs of cases against major corporate players – a political decision with a small or large 'p'; and

2. regulatory concern about collateral damage which might affect financial stability, not just of the Bank itself but also of its depositors and counterparties, generating systemic anxiety in the jurisdiction of sanction and elsewhere.

There is also a fear of undermining national businesses and unintentionally giving succour to foreign ones, which can mean under-supervising and under-enforcing violations, whether by banks, natural resources companies or professional services/accounting firms that are already highly concentrated. The extension of liability for bribery overseas, for example, in the *Bribery Act 2010* (UK) and the *Foreign Corrupt Practices Act of 1977*, 15 USC §§ 78dd – 1 – 78dd – 3 (1977), has been to extend bank liability for offending by their customers in high-risk areas or, alternatively, to pressure banks into de-risking clients in such areas when the estimated profitability of the account makes it not worth holding the account.[53]

How then to respond? One of the difficulties for regulators is that political pressures are most intensively driven by scandal. Additionally, scandal is often generated by older behaviours coming to light. Bureaucratic,

---

53 David Artingstall et al, 'Drivers & Impacts of Derisking: A Study of Representative Views and Data in the UK, by John Howell & Co. Ltd. for the Financial Conduct Authority' (Report, John Howell & Co Ltd, February 2016).

personal and political survival can get in the way of serious assessments of contemporary and future detriments and risks. On the other hand, without such pressures, regulators and law enforcement agencies may not be sufficiently alert or have the political courage, protection and resources to act. My own position is that, although we can weight the conflicting variables to get an outcome, this is an artificial pseudo-mathematical economics process and the true problem for decision-making lies in how to 'satisfice' the different objectives of reducing consumer detriment, increasing public confidence in control and satisfaction with the enhanced integrity of the financial sector, and retaining the dynamism and profitability of the sector to an acceptable level. This is an enormous societal challenge because, although (to take only one example from regulated activity) the rhetoric of anti-money laundering is to *preserve* the integrity of financial services, the defects in that integrity have become all too apparent in the evidence presented to the Royal Commission. Hence, preserving that is not a wholly desirable aim. On the other hand, it is unclear what level of various forms of commercial misconduct is acceptable (and to whom, domestically and internationally) or how we should properly apply cost-benefit analysis to the arena of crime control generally and white-collar crimes in particular.

Though concluding (perhaps correctly) that measuring culture in financial services was too difficult,[54] the UK Financial Conduct Authority has been encouraging some thinking about how to measure some forms of misconduct and enhancing the evidence base for the effects of some of its public-facing interventions.[55] It is important to appreciate that this is not a

---

54 The challenge was left to the elite Banking Standards Board, created in 2015 as a private sector body funded by membership subscriptions: see Banking Standards Board, 'Annual Review 2017/2018' (Report, Banking Standards Board, 2018).

55 Financial Conduct Authority, 'When and How We Use Field Trials' (Guidance, Financial Conduct Authority, July 2018); Financial Conduct Authority, 'How We Analyse the Costs and Benefits of Our Policies' (Guidance, Financial Conduct Authority, July 2018); William Lee, 'Estimating the Benefits of Interventions that Affect Consumer Behaviour' (Occasional Paper No 39, Financial Conduct Authority, July 2018). Mystery shopping field trials are an additional important measure: see Michael G. Findley, Daniel L. Nielson and J. C. Sharman, *Global Shell Games: Experiments in Transnational Relations, Crime, and Terrorism* (Cam-

mechanical process, however, especially where there is reasonable concern about the value of indicators as proxies for underlying detriment, not only in anti-money laundering,[56] but also in other less visible forms of market misconduct; some of which may be more important than the more visible ones analysed in the FCA work above. Thus, unless actively countered, a paradoxical effect may be of diverting regulation and even criminal enforcement towards those activities that can be more easily measured and for which intelligence sources already exist.

The FCA is re-examining its market cleanliness measurement in light of the rising trend in pre-announcement share price movements to 22 per cent in 2017 (though much lower than 30 per cent in 2009).[57] Measuring the success of crime and cybercrime prevention campaigns by one-time website clicks is a particularly inadequate measurement, though a low percentage click rate may be a good measure of failure. In regulatory actions, speed of intervention to reduce harm is a good way of thinking, provided there are not too many false positives. Regulators, however, should always be aware of the need to manage media and political pushback from individual cases that 'go wrong'.

V. Conclusions

There may come a day when, aping the gladiators of Rome before their Emperor, bank directors or management staff (rather than 'rogue traders') who reach their air-conditioned offices in Sydney will bow towards the Australian criminal courts and intone *incarceraturi te salutant*: 'those who are about to be jailed salute you'. But it is not clear how we could, in practice, calibrate sanctions so as to satisfice, if not satisfy, feelings of reasonable equity between harmfulness, wrongfulness and punishment for

bridge University Press, 2014) for an example of this, applied to global AML efforts between strangers.

56 Michael Levi, Peter Reuter and Terence Halliday, 'Can the AML System Be Evaluated without Better Data?' (2018) 69(2) *Crime, Law and Social Change* 307.

57 Financial Conduct Authority 'Annual Report and Accounts 2017/18 (for the year ended 31 March 2018)' (Report No HC 1202, Financial Conduct Authority, 19 July 2018) 37.

companies and their directors. I share the scepticism of some Australian academic commentators towards the use of criminal sanctions in areas such as cartels, insider trading and money laundering, and their search for more meaningful and less symbolic controls.[58]

So, where does this leave the issue of legitimacy? Bottoms and Tankebe propose three avenues for future work on legitimacy: studying power-holder legitimacy, measuring audience legitimacy, and developing longitudinal research on legitimacy (and the dialogic relationships between these three components).[59] They also note the distinction between legitimacy, focused on the present, and trust, focused on expectations about the future. This is directly relevant to this chapter. A publication six years old, however, is a long time ago in terms of social media developments, and one important issue to take on board now is the greater volatility which has been generated by the rise of social media, even attempting to set aside the issues of detected and undetected trolling, disinformation and misinformation, also known as 'fake news'. This makes it difficult to work out what is a rational mechanism for responding to real world problems, for fake news can have as powerful *political* effects as real news.

First, almost all of the legitimacy literature assumes a highly unequal power and social status relationship between power-holders and audiences, including offenders. This is not the case for the areas of market misconduct

---

58 For recent work, see, for example: Caron Beaton-Wells and Julie N. Clarke, 'Corporate Financial Penalties for Cartel Conduct in Australia: A Critique' (Paper, Beaton-Wells and Clarke, 2018); Helen Bird and George Gilligan, 'Deterring Corporate Wrongdoing: Penalties, Financial Services Misconduct and the Corporations Act 2001 (Cth)' (2016) 34 *Company and Securities Law Journal* 332; David Chaikin, 'A Critical Analysis of the Effectiveness of Anti-Money Laundering Measures with Reference to Australia' in Colin King, Clive Walker and Jimmy Gurulé (eds.), *The Palgrave Handbook of Criminal and Terrorism Financing Law* (Palgrave Macmillan, Cham, 2018) 293; Brent Fisse, 'Redress Facilitation Orders as a Sanction against Corporations' (2018) 37(1) *University of Queensland Law Journal* 85; Pamela F Hanrahan, 'Deterring White-Collar Crime: Insights from Australia's Insider Trading Penalties Regime (2017) 11(2-3) *Law and Financial Markets Review* 61.

59 Anthony Bottoms and Justice Tankebe, 'Beyond Procedural Justice: A Dialogic Approach to Legitimacy in Criminal Justice' (2012) 102(1) *Journal of Criminal Law and Criminology* 119, 160.

analysed here. The targets of police, and regulatory, investigation and action may have significantly higher status (though not always more social or legal networked power) than do the authorities. And much of the decision-making about who is to be deemed criminal and who merely guilty of 'misconduct' or 'mis-selling' takes place in private, hard-to-audit spaces, with the effects as well as intentions being capable of multiple alternative accounts of culpability and even of harm. Variations in approaches to elite misconduct in different advanced capitalist economies may tell us something about legitimacy needs in different countries. The extraordinary rapidity with which the UK government's 'independent body' in 2011 stripped the knighthood from the financial folk devil, former RBS CEO 'Sir' 'Fred the Shred'[60] Goodwin, showed the desire to bend before public wrath at 'unjust deserts'. As several outraged commentators noted, however, there was not a clear rationale for doing so, and other executive and non-executive directors of RBS who had misconducted themselves had been allowed to keep their titles.[61] The risk to his knighthood was used as leverage to persuade Sir Philip Green to repay a substantial proportion of the pension fund losses in BHS that he had sought to shift to its purchaser.[62] The Australian Government has a modified version of this, with the stripping of Orders of Australia from some businesspeople and judges, though only after

---

60 A sobriquet which might have sounded gangster-like applied to an underworld figure, but which resounded positively at the time to shareholders seeking a reduction in 'head count' to generate higher profits.

61 See Treasury Committee, *The FSA's Report into the Failure of RBS*, House of Commons Paper No 5, Session 2012–13 (2012). In 2013, there was similar debate about the titles and entitlement to work in the financial services industry of the former heads of HBOS, whose reckless lending policies resulted in an ill-judged take over by Lloyds, in an agreement brokered by the Labour government, which later spent £20 billion on a still controversial and litigated bail-out for Lloyds. Under Parliamentary and media pressure, Sir James Crosby (who had also been Deputy Chair of the Financial Services Authority) voluntarily resigned his knighthood (which had never been done before) and took a cut in his generous pension arrangements to reflect his admitted culpability. The other directors did nothing.

62 David Nelken and Michael Levi, 'Sir Philip Green and the Unacceptable Face of Capitalism' (2018) 29(1) *King's Law Journal* 1.

conviction or on the eve of their *criminal* trials.[63] Though some lost their jobs or bonuses following Royal Commission revelations, it is too early to assess whether there has been a genuine sea change in Australia. Many private internal reviews have taken place (whose adequacy may be assessed by ASIC, AUSTRAC and other regulators). But whether they are genuine *and competent* attempts to assess contemporary financial crime and money laundering risks, rather than primarily to deal with public and regulatory risks, is unknown. While the market misconduct and money laundering risks may be global, the close ties of Australia to the Asian markets may give rise to more accented risks than elsewhere.

By contrast, looking at the efforts some Swiss have made to take on transnational bribery cases from the developing world as domestic money laundering cases, it appears that the Swiss had a greater need for legitimacy, at least to avoid clampdowns on their banking and tax secrecy by other OECD countries. The (now retired) proactive Geneva magistrate, M. Bernard Bertossa, a socialist, agreed with amusement to my proposition that, if he had not existed, Switzerland would have had to invent him.[64] Time will tell what levels of activism against corrupt public officials will be displayed by an EU-level public prosecutor, whose powers and independence of member state consent to action have been significantly neutralised by the European Council. The outcome of the Australian Royal Commission and pressures for a specialist Commonwealth anti-corruption agency remains unclear at this point in time. Whilst some might think that legitimacy is institutionally inscribed, this chapter shows that perceptions of fairness are at least as important a source of legitimacy. The chapter finds its criminal justice manifestation dependent on the autonomy of

---

63 Eoin Blackwell, *Alan Bond, Eddie Obeid, Brian Burke and the Other Men Stripped of Their Australia Day Honours* (24 January 2015) news.com.au <https://www.news.com.au/national/alan-bond-eddie-obeid-brian-burke-and-the-other-men-stripped-of-their-australia-day-honours/news-story/91dc3ed9f00f49e71407089a-ecd211ef>. We do not know whether they contemplated disgrace at the time they committed their offences: if they did, then this was not a deterrent for *them*, though it may have been for others. But to be deterred by such a sanction, one must first have the honours or an expectation of getting one.

64 Interview with M. Bernard Bertossa (2002).

investigators and prosecutors from political decisions, and on the activism and competence of those authorities, using investigation tools that are not always well designed to deal with transnational cases. The legitimacy of both the prosecutions and the non-prosecutions of elite businesspeople looks very different in: Rudd, Abbott, Turnbull and Morrison's Australia; Putin's Russia; Xi Jinping's China; Blair, Cameron and May's England and Wales; and Bush, Obama and Trump's USA.

Finally, the search for rationality in regulation remains elusive, as the costs of being inaccurate can be high, in the direction of both underestimating and overestimating the level of internal misconduct and external risk. In an open society, the harms framework, and the methods by which risks are to be assessed, *should* be open to public and professional debate, even though the judgments made about the riskiness of individual institutions and persons should *not* be and realistically cannot be.[65] This all requires a level of media and political maturity that are not always present, but must be striven for. The divergence between criminologists and regulation scholars is partly a matter of language and focus, but credible deterrence requires a good understanding of organisational and political culture. Enhancing our understanding of that is a good preliminary step to financial harm reduction. Balancing values is a political decision, but acting upon such empirical insights demands a collective willingness to adopt evidence-informed strategies and that is a challenge throughout the world.

Chapter 7

Banks, New Technologies and the International Standards Against Money Laundering and Terrorist Financing

Gordon Hook

> Gaping holes in the anti-money laundering systems of Australia's big banks are being exploited by crime groups to wash up to $5 million in drug cash a day, according to confidential briefings by federal and state policing agencies.[1]

Introduction

If as an Australian you were stunned at the 2017 comment in the epigraph, as no doubt most readers were, banks were equally stunned. If it is true that $5 million day (or over $1.8 billion a year) is being 'washed' or laundered through banks from illegal drug transactions alone, how much more in other criminal proceeds from fraud, tax evasion, theft, insider trading, etc., is making its way into our banks? And not just banks! What about other financial institutions such as security dealers, credit unions, money value transfer services and others? And, what about non-bank entities such as lawyers, accountants, real estate agents and casinos that use the services and products of banks and other financial institutions on behalf of their clients and customers? Are they also being exploited by criminals?

---

1   Nick McKenzie, Richard Baker and Georgina Mitchell, 'It's Not Just CBA: All the Banks are Exposed to Millions in Money Laundering', *Sydney Morning Herald* (online), 14 September 2017 <https://www.smh.com.au/business/banking-and-finance/its-not-just-cba-all-the-banks-are-exposed-to-millions-in-money-laundering-20170914-gyhhpi.html.>

Banks went scurrying to check their anti-money laundering systems[2] with the recent news burning in their minds that, just prior to the media comment cited in the epigraph, the Australian regulator responsible for supervising banks in relation to their anti-money laundering systems (AUSTRAC) had filed a claim in the High Court against the Commonwealth Bank of Australia alleging an enormous number of failures (over 53,500) in its cash threshold[3] and suspicious transaction[4] monitoring and reporting system.

Banks play a central, if not the pivotal, role in any country's economy. For instance, [banks hold] the majority of financial system assets. In addition to traditional retail deposit-taking and lending activities, banks are involved in almost all other facets of financial intermediation, including business banking, trading in financial markets, stockbroking, insurance and funds management.[5]

The banking industry facilitates transactions between individuals, commercial enterprises and governments, and is a source of credit which drives economies towards greater wealth. Banks deal almost entirely in money (in various forms) and as such are inherently at risk of exploitation by criminals, terrorists and customers who are neither, but who may be willing to exploit bank errors when an opportunity arises.[6] Given the inherent risk of exploitation, banks need to impose controls to reduce their

---

2   National Australia Bank, Annual Report 2017, p. 108 issued November 2017: 'It is possible that, as the work progresses [AML/CFT review], further issues may be identified and additional strengthening may be required. The outcomes of the investigation and remediation process for specific issues identified to date, and for any issues identified in the future, are uncertain' <https://www.nab.com.au/content/dam/nabrwd/About-Us/shareholder-centre/documents/2017-annual-financial-report.pdf>.

3   Cash transactions of $10,000 or more.

4   Cash transactions of any amount (even very small transactions) that give rise to a suspicion that the funds are the proceeds of crime.

5   Reserve Bank of Australia, 'The Structure of the Australian Financial System' *Financial Stability Review*, March 2006 <https://www.rba.gov.au/publications/fsr/2006/mar/struct-aus-fin-sys.html>.

6   For instance, withdrawing funds from their accounts placed there in error by the bank but claiming them as their own.

vulnerabilities and manage their residual risk. Usually these measures are required by law but in some cases go well beyond legal and regulatory requirements.

A quick Google search of 'banks and money laundering' reveals no shortage of cases around the world where banks have been fined or other action taken for breaches of their own anti-money laundering and counter-financing of terrorism ('AML/CFT') policies.

This chapter looks at the Financial Action Task Force (FATF) Recommendations[7] as they relate to banks. More specifically, it will focus on the FATF standards that require countries to address the risks of money laundering and terrorist financing posed by new technologies and it will link that discussion to the Commonwealth Bank of Australia case just mentioned. Prior to that, the chapter will outline the status of the FATF Recommendations.

I. Are the FATF 'Recommendations' Mandatory?

The FATF's 40 Recommendations are widely recognised as the global benchmark for AML/CFT. The suite of those Recommendations contains seven parts addressing a range of wide-sweeping policy areas, including criminal law, private-sector regulation and international cooperation. At their core, they require countries to:[8]

- criminalise money laundering and terrorist financing;
- confiscate the proceeds of crime;
- freeze terrorist assets and implement measures relating to proliferation financing;
- supervise financial institutions and other reporting entities to ensure compliance with customer due

---

7   Financial Action Task Force, International Standards on Combating Money Laundering and the Financing of Terrorism & Proliferation: The FATF Recommendations (FATF Recommendations), October 2018 <http://www.fatf-gafi.org>.

8   See Financial Action Task Force (FATF) website <http://www.fatf-gafi.org> for comprehensive information on FATF standards relating to money laundering and terrorist financing.

diligence and other preventative measures;

- implement measures relating to politically exposed persons (both domestic and foreign); and
- cooperate effectively with other countries given the transnational dimension to money laundering, terrorist financing and proliferation financing.

'Countries' are required to take these measures which, in turn, means that where the FATF Recommendations are clear on requiring legislation, law-makers must impose obligations on financial and non-financial institutions as well as other private sector entities to comply with certain recommendations and, in doing so, impose significant regulatory and cost burdens on those entities, and also on government agencies. Noting that burden, many senior executives in the private sector as well as government policy advisers have often asked whether the FATF Recommendations are actually mandatory or 'just recommendations'; after all, that is what they are called. Why not simply treat them as *suggestions* or *best practice,* and leave countries to enact laws to address their own circumstances, and financial institutions to determine the range, scope and content of institutional measures to address their specific risks?

The short answer is that the FATF Recommendations *are* mandatory. There are a number of reasons supporting this conclusion.

First (the weaker of the points), in 2005, the UN Security Council, acting under Chapter VII of the *Charter of the United Nations,* strongly urged countries to comply with the FATF Recommendations.[9] Resolutions issued under Chapter VII of the *Charter of the United Nations* are considered legally binding on UN member states under Article 25. Within that context, the UN has sent a strong message that countries should implement the FATF Recommendations to address a serious issue relating to the maintenance of international peace and security. When used in the

9   *Threats to International Peace and Security Caused by Terrorist Acts* SC Res 1617, UN Doc S/RES/1617 (29 July 2005) para 7: '[The Council] *Strongly urges* all Member States to implement the comprehensive international standards embodied in the Financial Action Task Force's (FATF) Forty Recommendations.'

context of a Chapter VII Resolution, the term 'strongly urges' borders on meaning 'obligated to implement'.

Second (the more compelling reason), just as a country voluntarily assumes the obligations contained in a treaty or international convention, countries voluntarily assume the obligation to enact laws and other measures to give effect to the FATF Recommendations as a pre-condition to joining one of the FATF-style Regional Bodies (FSRBs) around the world. While voluntary assumption of this obligation does not take the form of signing a treaty and ratifying that instrument in the national legislature, it does involve issuing a letter by a Minister which includes a statement from that Minister that the country applying commits to implementing the full range of FATF Recommendations, without reservation.

Moreover (as a third point), the FATF and FSRBs have compliance mechanisms in place to enforce the obligations voluntarily assumed by each country. Failure to comply with the obligations can result in 'membership action'[10] which may include action up to, and including, termination of membership of the organisation. One of the FATF's own compliance mechanisms is the public listing process conducted by its working group called the 'International Cooperation Review Group' (ICRG). The various lists adopted by the FATF on the advice of this group include the *grey list*, *black list* and *counter-measures list*.[11] Without going into the details of the process and its underlying policies, it has been a tremendously successful process in moving countries with AML/CFT deficiencies to greater compliance levels. Regulators, financial and non-financial institutions worldwide, have paid increasing attention to these lists since they were first

---

10 In the Asia/Pacific Group on Money Laundering, membership action includes a range of responses from the organisation including, at the lower end, requiring the country to report regularly on its efforts to comply; to issuing a public statement on the country's deficiencies alerting the public, including financial institutions, to note those deficiencies; to the most severe remedy of membership termination. See: Asia/Pacific Group on Money Laundering, *APG Terms of Reference 2012* (Terms of Reference, 20 September 2018) 8.

11 The FATF website lists countries in these categories under 'High Risk and Other Monitored Jurisdictions'. See: Financial Action Task Force, *High-Risk and Other Monitored Jurisdictions* (2018) <http://www.fatf-gafi.org/countries/#high-risk>.

established in 2009, and made significant commercial and other decisions as a result of a country's listing. Some of the actions taken have included denial of financial services by the banking sector in a non-listed country (for instance, correspondent banking services) against the banks in a listed country.

And the fourth (and final point) which sets the enforceability of the FATF Recommendations on a stronger footing than a treaty or convention obligation is that, even if a country is not a member of the FATF or a FSRB, and, therefore, has not issued a letter from one of its Ministers to voluntarily assume the obligations noted, the ICRG-compliance-focused process in the FATF, nevertheless, applies to those countries.[12] The same applies to a country which has had its membership in a FSRB terminated (as mentioned above).[13] Indeed, a country in those circumstances (terminated membership) would be more likely self-referred by the FATF to its own ICRG process, than not. So it is no comfort to a country that, after committing to implement the full range of FATF Recommendations, decides to terminate its membership in the FSRB or, worse, has its membership terminated by the FSRB itself for failing to meet its membership obligations. Pressure imposed by the FATF's ICRG listing mechanism may continue to apply. In other words, to quote American boxer Joe Louis: 'You can run but you cannot hide'. This arguably sets the enforceability of the Recommendations on a stronger footing than

---

12 One of the referral criteria that the FATF takes into account in deciding whether to publicly list a country is the non-membership of that country in an FSRB. Non-membership in such a body is, alone, a reason to list. See: FATF, *ICRG Procedures for 4th Round of Mutual Evaluations* (Financial Action Task Force Document No FATF/PLEN/RD(2016)4/FINAL, [2(a)]. However, other factors may impact the FATF's decision. For instance, the size of assets in a country's financial sector is a factor. Some countries in the Pacific that are not FSRB-members, but whose financial sector is so small that entry into the ICRG process may not be necessary as the risk those countries pose is small to negligible. On the other hand, North Korea is not a member of an FSRB. Since the threat it poses to the international financial system is significant, for a variety of reasons, it is subject to ICRG monitoring.

13 No country up to the end of 2018 had its membership in the FATF or a FSRB terminated for failure to comply with their obligations (although some countries have come close).

enforceability of a treaty or a UN Convention which requires being a party to these instruments for them to be enforced.

There are other similarities between the FATF Recommendations, on the one hand, and treaty-based instruments, on the other. But, suffice it to say that, despite nomenclature, the FATF Recommendations are not merely *recommendations* in the common use of that word, but binding and enforceable *obligations*.

II. Identifying and Managing Risks of Criminal Exploitation

The FATF Recommendations contain a number of measures targeted at 'reporting entities', including banks, requiring them to mitigate their inherent and residual risk of exploitation for money laundering and terrorist financing, and to prevent criminals from using their services. Those measures include requiring banks to:

1. assess the financial crime risks of their products, customers and delivery channels;
2. implement preventative measures (as defined in the FATF Recommendations) to address the varying levels of risk identified, referred to as the risk-based approach; and
3. implement measures to require suspicious transactions and threshold cash transactions (cash transactions of at least $10 000) to be reported to a competent government authority.
4. The Recommendations also require countries to:
5. implement measures to ensure that competent authorities supervise banks for compliance with these obligations; and
6. provide a range of effective sanctions available for those authorities to impose on banks who fail to comply with their own policies.

A. Risk Assessment (Part A)

Generally speaking, as one author put it, 'risk is the effect of uncertainty on specific objectives'.[14] When this concept is applied to criminal offences that generate illicit funds, a bank faces the risk of money laundering if it either lacks or does not understand, the nature and scope of controls within its operating environment to address the possibility of abuse by criminals or the financing of terrorists, terrorist groups or terrorist acts.

As stated at the beginning of the chapter, banks are inherently vulnerable to money laundering and terrorist financing. Vulnerabilities are extant at varying levels through a number of services and delivery channels. FATF Recommendation 1 requires banks to assess their own risk across various products offered, services delivered, delivery channels and clients, and then put measures in place to address those risks. What is left after application of those measures is residual risk of varying degrees and levels. Some residual risks will be low while others will remain higher and present challenges to banks to manage and address. Those higher residual risks may be found in deposit-taking, lending, foreign exchange, money value and transfer services, correspondent banking, ATMs, etc., and through various types of customers including domestic and foreign politically exposed persons, clients from high-risk jurisdictions and clients whose names appear on watch lists, such as the Specially Designated Nationals List (maintained by the United States Office on Foreign Assets and Control)[15] and various UN sanctions lists, such as Al Qaeda terrorists, organisations and associated entities listed pursuant to UN Security Council Resolution 1267, and its successor Resolutions.

Banks are further required to adopt a risk-based approach to their management of varying levels of identified risk.[16] In Australia, these requirements have been included in the *Anti-Money Laundering and*

---

14 MD Masud Rana, *Anti Money Laundering and Counter Financing of Terrorism Compliance* (Chandrabati Academy, 2018) 53

15 'The Office of Foreign Asset Control, or 'OFAC' as it commonly referred to in financial sectors, is part of the US Treasury Department.

16 FATF Recommendations, above n 7; 8, 29–31.

Counter-Terrorism Financing Act 2006 ('*AML/CFT Act*')[17] under sections 84-6 and 165. Parts 8.1 and 9.1 of the *AML/CTF Rules* further require banks to produce a written programme to identify, mitigate and manage their risks. For higher residual risk, banks must direct more effort at addressing the issue compared to lower risk areas.

Understanding risk is the fundamental basis for the effective mitigation of institution-related risk. In any scenario where a bank or other type of financial institution fails to undertake a comprehensive risk assessment across its services, products, delivery channels and types of clients, or where it does so, but, nevertheless, fails to understand its risk, the bank or institution will no doubt run afoul of the regulatory burden imposed on it by law.

B. Preventative Measures (Part D)

Some of the measures required by the FATF to reduce risk are referred to as 'preventative measures' under Part D of the FATF Recommendations. They include programmes relating to:

- customer due diligence (R 10);
- record keeping (R 11);
- politically exposed persons (R 12);
- correspondent banking (R 13);
- new technologies (R 15); and
- suspicious transaction reporting (R 20).

Recommendations 10, 11 and 20 are required to be spelled out in legislation while the others listed can be contained in 'enforceable means' that are legal instruments (including regulations) that carry penalties for non-compliance.[18] Recommendation 10 on customer due diligence has

---

17 AML/CFT Act s 165.

18 FATF Recommendations, above n 14, 108 – *Legal Basis of Requirements on Financial Institutions and DNFBPs*. Paragraph 2 provides that: '... *law* refers to any legislation issued or approved through a Parliamentary process or other

proven to be one of the most difficult recommendations in the suite for financial institutions to implement, primarily because of the requirements around identification of 'beneficial owners' as defined in the standards. The definition is deceptively simple yet inherently difficult to implement.[19]

C. Supervision (Part F)

A number of the FATF Recommendations require countries to implement legal and regulatory measures in relation to the supervision of banks. The relevant Recommendations are:

- R 26: Regulation and supervision of financial institutions;
- R 27: Powers of supervisors;
- R 34: Guidance and feedback; and
- R 35: Sanctions.

Some of the requirements of Recommendation 26 (supervision) are that banks must have market entry controls, licence requirements and conduct on- and off-site supervision. There is, however, no 'one-size-fits-all' supervision model which is required, or even recommended, by the FATF when it comes to Recommendation 26. The principal guiding requirement is that banks should conduct supervision on the basis of a risk-based approach driven by their own institutional risk assessments, informed in turn by national risk assessments, whether at the financial sector level or more generally. The adoption of an AML/CFT supervisory model by any specific country, involving one or more sector supervisors, is a 'national

---

equivalent means ... which imposes mandatory requirements with sanctions for non-compliance'. Paragraph 3 states that: *'enforceable means* refers to regulations, guidelines, instructions or other documents or mechanisms that set out enforceable AML/CFT requirements in mandatory language with sanctions for non-compliance, and which are issued or approved by a competent authority'.

19 FATF Recommendations, above n 14, 111: *'Beneficial owner* refers to the natural person(s) who ultimately owns or controls a customer and/or the natural person on whose behalf a transaction is being conducted. It also includes those persons who exercise ultimate effective control over a legal person or arrangement'.

decision that should be adopted taking into consideration the structure and risk of the financial sector in each country'.[20]

As mentioned at the outset, while the FATF Recommendations are uniquely binding obligations, the various sets of Recommendations and their assessment-related sub-criteria used to evaluate compliance are not so prescriptive or rigid such that there is only one way to achieve the policy compliance-objective. Different institutional arrangements, depending on the risk and context of each jurisdiction, are permissible so long as they address the circumstances of the country concerned and meet the overall policy objectives of the FATF standards.

III. FATF Standards on New Technologies

FATF Recommendation 15 requires countries and financial institutions to identify and assess the risk of money laundering and terrorist financing with respect to new products, new business practices, new delivery mechanisms and the use of new or developing technologies for both new and pre-existing products.

Rapid changes in technology, including developments in artificial intelligence and biometrics, have brought a host of new products and services to the banking industry, including but not limited to:

- blockchain technology;
- digital currency;
- application programming interfaces;
- mobile and digital banking;
- smart ATMs;
- new forms of security authentication; and
- 'internet of things' or IoT.[21]

---

20 Financial Action Task Force, Guidance for a Risk-Based Approach: Effective Supervision and Enforcement by AML/CFT Supervisors of the Financial Sector and Law Enforcement (Guidance, Financial Action Task Force, October 2015) 5.

21 Phil Goldstein, *5 Trends to Watch in Banking Technology in 2018* (21 December 2018) BizTech <https://biztechmagazine.com/article/2017/12/5-trends-watch-banking-technology-2018>.

Each of these technologies, when utilised in the banking sector for processes including client on-boarding, transaction monitoring, reporting and management,[22] poses its own unique risks of money laundering and terrorist financing.[23] As one author put it, new technologies 'are better than cash for moving large sums of money; non-face to face business relationships favour the use of straw buyers and false identities; the absence of credit risk discourages service providers from obtaining complete and accurate customer information'.[24]

Recommendation 15 is inserted in Part D of the FATF Recommendations as a 'Preventative Measure'. The recommendation, however, actually has nothing to do with 'preventative measures' in the sense in which the FATF uses that term and more to do with risk assessments as required under Part A, Recommendation 1, which is about policies and coordination (a point of importance to bear in mind for later). Recommendation 15 reads as follows:

> Countries and financial institutions should identify and assess the money laundering or terrorist financing risks that may arise in relation to (a) the development of new products and new business practices, including new delivery mechanisms, and (b) the use of new or developing technologies for both new and pre-existing products. In the case of financial institutions, such a risk assessment should take place prior to the launch of the new products, business practices or the use of new or developing technologies. They should take appropriate measures to manage and mitigate those risks.[25]

22 See, Financial Conduct Authority, 'New Technologies and Anti-Money Launder-ing Compliance' (Report, Financial Conduct Authority, 31 March 2017).

23 Money laundering risks relating to digital or virtual currencies are discussed in David Chaikin and Derwent Coshott (eds.), *Digital Disruption* (Melbourne: Australian Scholarly Publishing, 2017).

24 Miguel Abel Souto, 'Money Laundering, New Technologies, FATF and Spanish Penal Reform' (2013) 16(3) *Journal of Money Laundering Control* 266.

25 FATF Recommendations, above n 14, 15.

This two-pronged Recommendation requires countries (as part of their national risk assessment exercise) and financial institutions to: (1) undertake risk assessments relating to new products, businesses and delivery mechanisms; and (2) in relation to financial institutions undertake those assessments prior to launching the new technologies. Curiously, the FATF assessment methodology, which is designed to put an evaluation framework around the key points of the Recommendation, subtly alters the wording of the Recommendation to read as follows:

> 15.1 Countries and financial institutions should identify and assess the ML and TF risks that may arise in relation to the development of new products and new business practices, including new delivery mechanisms, and the use of new or developing technologies for both new and pre-existing products.
>
> 15.2 Financial institutions *should be required to*:
>> (a) undertake the risk assessments prior to the launch or use of such products, practices and technologies; and
>> (b) take appropriate measures to manage and mitigate the risks.[26]

Recalling that, where the FATF Recommendations are clear on requiring legislation, lawmakers must impose obligations on financial and non-financial institutions to comply with certain recommendations, the section underlined in criterion 15.2 adds a new and arguably *ultra vires* step (not in Recommendation 15) of requiring laws, regulations or other means that are enforceable at law to compel financial institutions to undertake risk assessments. In and of itself, this may not be problematic but what is curious, still, is that assessment reports published by the FATF have consequently shifted the focus away from whether financial institutions have *actually*

---

26 Financial Action Task Force, Methodology for Assessing Technical Compliance with the FATF Recommendations and the Effectiveness of AML/CFT Systems (FATF Assessment Methodology, October 2018) 52.

undertaken the required assessment to whether financial institutions are *simply required to* do it by law. Countries are therefore receiving credit by the FATF for having a law in place even though the action required under that law has not been undertaken. Conversely, in countries where financial institutions have undertaken risk assessments, but not compelled by law to do so, no credit is being given. It has come to the point now with FATF evaluation exercises that, once FATF teams determine whether a law is in place to require risk assessments, their evaluation process for determining compliance with Recommendations 15 seems to end. The words 'seem to end' are used because, in many of the evaluation reports, there does not appear to be a discussion or even passing reference to whether the action has been undertaken. Whether FATF evaluation teams have even looked at the issue cannot be determined but it must be assumed that they have not.[27]

Moreover, this unique approach has been applied to criterion 15.1, even though the wording is not in the Recommendation itself and even though the assessment methodology does not contain the words. The FATF is assigning 'pass marks'[28] to countries for simply requiring themselves and financial institutions to undertake risk assessments even if no national or financial institution-level new technology risk assessments have actually been carried out. The precedent set by the FATF means that, with respect to this sub-criterion, evaluation reports have gravitated away from a product-focus to a simple enquiry whether countries and financial institutions are compelled by legislation or other law to undertake the assessment relevant to that sub-criterion.[29] The significance of this will be clear in a moment.

---

27 Only one report so far (in 2018) seems to have properly applied the methodology. That is the recently published report on Palau by the APG. See APG (2018), *Anti-money laundering and counter-terrorist financing measures – Palau,* Third Round Mutual Evaluation Report, APG, Sydney, 124 <http://www.apgml.org/includes/handlers/get-document.ashx?d=2c0cc104-d8ea-491d-8815-24cf78104604>: 'There are no requirements in Palau that require FIs [financial institutions] to identify and assess the ML/TF risks related to new technologies ... Nevertheless, the three US banks (that contribute to approx. 98% of the financial activity) do in practice undertake risk assessments of new products including new technologies which apply to the branches they manage in Palau'.

28 'Pass marks' are either 'largely compliant' or 'compliant' ratings.

29 Only one non-FATF assessment has actually properly applied the Recommenda-

Before closing off this discussion, it is important to reflect on whether FATF Immediate Outcome 1 (IO 1) covers the point just addressed. That outcome requires that '[m]oney laundering and terrorist financing risks are understood and, where appropriate, action coordinated domestically to combat money laundering and the financing of terrorism'. The question one might ask is that, even if the FATF has, by its methodology of assessment and precedent of decisions, reduced the meaning of the two sub-criteria in the manner discussed, perhaps evaluation reports relating to IO 1 address whether risk assessments under Recommendations 15 have been undertaken. The short answer is that none of the core issues under IO 1 address the point and it appears that none of the FATF country reports relating to IO 1 address whether, in fact, such new technology risk assessments are undertaken by financial institutions. The assessment report of Denmark comes close, but not in relation to IO 1. In the discussion of IO 4 (dealing with the application of preventive measures on the basis of risk), the following comment is made:[30]

> Although Denmark's financial system is technologically advanced, there are no explicit obligations over risks presented by new technologies. The largest banks and casinos indicated that significant scrutiny is given to new technologies, but it did not appear that the scrutiny was done in the context of mitigating ML/TF risks. Only one [financial institution] interviewed identified pre-paid cards and some internet payment systems as higher-risk technology. Most of the risk assessments provided to assessors were rather basic and did not cover risks relating to new technologies such as mobile

---

tion in its plain meaning. See: APG (2018), *Anti-money laundering and counter-terrorist financing measures – Palau,* Third Round Mutual Evaluation Report, APG, Sydney <www.apgml.org/includes/handlers/get-document.ashx?d=2c-0cc104-d8ea-491d-8815-24cf78104604>.

30 FATF (2017), *Anti-money laundering and counter-terrorist financing measures – Denmark,* Fourth Round Mutual Evaluation Report, FATF, Paris, 95 <www.fatf-gafi.org/publications/mutualevaluations/documents/mer-denmark-2017.html>.

payment. It is thus unclear whether the banking or other sectors are aware of these ML/TF risks, despite Denmark moving towards a cashless society and being among the first countries to use new information technologies (e.g. instant payments).

Other FATF reports have made similar passing comments in relation to IOs other than IO 1 but none seem to have addressed the explicit obligation in the FATF Recommendations to determine whether risk assessments for new or emerging technologies have actually been done by financial institutions. This is likely a function of the fact, noted earlier in this chapter, that Recommendation 15, though contained in Part D of the suite of recommendations dealing with 'Preventative Measures', actually should have been inserted in Part A dealing specifically with 'Risk Assessments' and risk-related policies.

IV. Banks, New Technologies, Money Laundering and Risk

Returning to the Commonwealth Bank of Australia (CBA) case mentioned at the outset of this chapter, CBA is one of the largest banks in Australia and within the Asia-Pacific region. It has approximately 1,350 branches, 16.6 million customers, employs approximately 51,800 people and processes over 16 million transactions per day.[31] For the year ending 30 June 2017 it declared a net after-tax profit of $9.928 billion.[32]

In May 2012, the CBA introduced what they referred to as Intelligent Deposit Machines (IDMs) – a type of automated teller machine (ATM) which can accept cash and cheque deposits into CBA accounts. CBA cards as well as cards from other banks and financial institutions could be

---

31 Chief Executive Officer of the Australian Transaction Reports and Analysis Centre and Commonwealth Bank of Australia, 'Statement of Agreed Facts and Admissions' (Statement of Agreed Facts and Admissions No NSD1305 of 2017, Federal Court of Australia, 2018) 3 [11]-[13].

32 Commonwealth Bank of Australia, *Results* (2018) <https://www.commbank.com.au/about-us/shareholders/financial-information/results.html>.

used to deposit funds directly into the account of a CBA customer. Cash deposited through an IDM in bulk form, and not inserted individually note-by-note, is automatically counted by the IDM and instantly credited to the nominated beneficiary CBA account. Moreover, and without delay, those funds are then immediately available for transfer, including for international transfer, to off-shore accounts.[33]

Five years after the introduction of IDMs to the Australian consumer market, on 3 August 2017, AUSTRAC published a notice on its website stating that:

> Australia's financial intelligence and regulatory agency, AUSTRAC, today initiated civil penalty proceedings in the Federal Court against the Commonwealth Bank of Australia (CBA) for serious and systemic non-compliance with the *Anti-Money Laundering and Counter-Terrorism Financing Act 2006* (AML/CTF Act) ... [The] action follows an investigation by AUSTRAC into CBA's compliance, particularly regarding its use of intelligent deposit machines (IDMs). AUSTRAC's action alleges over 53,700 contraventions of the AML/CTF Act.

A year later in 2018, CBA and AUSTRAC agreed on a record-breaking civil penalty against CBA in the amount of $700 million.[34] The Notice of Filing in the Federal Court[35] alleged that the IDMs could process up to 200 notes of varying denominations per deposit. Since the largest note in Australia is the $100 note, individual IDMs could accept up to $20,000

---

33 Chief Executive Officer of the Australian Transaction Reports and Analysis Centre and Commonwealth Bank of Australia, above n 31, 6 [26].

34 Shane Wright, 'Commonwealth Bank to Pay Record $700 Million Fine over Use of ATM systems by Criminals, Terrorists', *The West Australian* (online), 4 June 2018 <https://thewest.com.au/business/banking/commonwealth-bank-to-pay-record-700-million-fine-over-use-of-atm-systems-by-criminals-terrorists-ng-b88855637z>.

35 Chief Executive Officer of the Australian Transaction Reports and Analysis Centre and Commonwealth Bank of Australia, above n 31.

per transaction. The 200-note cap on cash deposits only related to one IDM at a time, and so, by using multiple IDMs on the same day, there was no limit on the daily amount of cash a depositor could insert in the machines and have credited to their account. A limit is set only indirectly by the number of IDMs available at any given time.

Not long after their introduction, IDMs became very popular with a sharp rise in the amount of cash deposited in a short period of time:

- Between June 2012 and November 2012 (6 months), about $89.1 million in cash was deposited in IDMs;
- Between January 2016 and June 2016 (6 months), about $5.81 billion in cash was deposited in IDMs;
- In May and June 2016 alone, over $1 billion per month (or $2 billion) was deposited in IDMs;
- In May 2017, there were 805 IDMs in Australia and during that month alone cash deposits were approximately $1.7 billion.[36]

All of the transactions could have been, and many were, anonymous. Bank cards from institutions other than CBA could be used to deposit cash into CBA's IDMs without capturing customer identification data. A large number of reports, both threshold transaction reports (totalling 53,506 in number) and suspicious matter reports, were not filed in accordance with obligations under Australia's AML/CFT laws until a number of years later. The total value of the threshold transaction reports not filed within the time required by law was $624.7 million. Alleged by AUSTRAC was that 1,640 of those reports (with transaction values totalling $17.3 million) related to matters tied to a number of money laundering syndicates under investigation by law enforcement authorities. Six of those reports related to potential terrorism and terrorist financing risks (raising national security concerns).

An important part of the allegations against CBA was the failure

36 Ibid 7 [29].

of the bank to undertake a money laundering and terrorist financing risk assessment of its IDMs prior to their introduction to customers, and, thereafter, to implement an appropriate programme to mitigate the identified risks and vulnerabilities of that technology until a number of years later. CBA admitted its failure in this respect and consequently admitted failing to implement a risk mitigation programme by not, amongst other things, introducing daily limits on cash deposits until late 2017.

As pointed out above, there is a requirement in FATF Recommendation 15 to assess the risks of new technologies and take measures to implement risk mitigation programmes.[37] IDMs were a new technology and clearly had some characteristics that posed significant risks, including acceptance of cash by anonymous customers with no daily limit, upon which funds could be transferred immediately to offshore accounts (which occurred). Even if this risk was obvious without a formal assessment (as it clearly seems to be without much intellectual effort or consultation), no programme was established to address that risk. In 2018, the case against CBA was settled and implemented by way of a Federal Court Order, for a civil penalty of $700 million plus $2.5 million in costs – the largest corporate penalty in Australian history.

At this point, we will depart from the allegations and agreed statements of facts against CBA and look at some other relevant issues not widely reported in the media that link back to what was discussed earlier on by FATF Recommendation 15 in relation to new technologies.

At about the same time that the CBA's IDMs were being exploited by criminal syndicates, the FATF was undertaking a mutual evaluation of Australia's AML/CFT system against the FATF Recommendations, including Recommendation 15 discussed above. The initial stages of the evaluation began in early 2014 with a comprehensive on-site visit by an evaluation team of six international experts[38] over two weeks in August

---

37 FATF Recommendations, above n 14, 15.

38 The experts were selected from Singapore, Norway, United States, Netherlands, Hong Kong and the IMF. The team was supported by three FATF Secretariat staff members and two APG Secretariat staff members (including the author – however none of the information discussed in this chapter is drawn from

2014. Final publication of the report occurred in April 2015.[39]

The FATF evaluation team looked at a national threat assessment on money laundering, originally published in 2011 but released in a sanitised form for public consumption in late 2013.[40] It addressed to some extent the risks associated with new technologies – ATMs to be specific. The focus on ATM risks was however on 'merchant-filled ATMs'. That is, the risk that ATMs could be stuffed with illicit cash from criminal activity by *ATM licensees* and co-mingled with legitimate funds. The risk assessment articulates the concern more clearly by stating that funds withdrawn by unwitting customer-users standing at the ATM are withdrawn from the account in the customer's bank and transferred to the merchant's bank account after settlement, often the following day. The customer-user receives in hand the criminal funds, believing they are funds from their own account. The national threat assessment reported that '[a]lthough no cases involving money laundering through these systems have been identified in Australia to date, law enforcement and intelligence agencies in Australia and overseas identify these systems as a vulnerability'.[41]

Around the same time as the FATF evaluation team was considering material for the report on Australia, the Australian government released a public version of its terrorist financing risk assessment in 2014.[42] No concerns, however, were raised in that report relating to terrorist financing risk associated with ATMs or the recently-introduced IDMs. The focus of Australian authorities and, by implication, banks and other financial

non-public sources by the author).

39 FATF and APG (2015), *Anti-money laundering and counter-terrorist financing measures – Australia*, Fourth Round Mutual Evaluation Report, FATF, Paris and APG, Sydney <www.fatf-gafi.org/topics/mutualevaluations /documents/mer-australia-2015.html>.

40 Australian Transaction Reports and Analysis Centre, *National Threat Assessment on Money Laundering 2011* (Report, Australian Transaction Reports and Analysis Centre, 2011).

41 Australian Transaction Reports and Analysis Centre, *National Threat Assessment on Money Laundering 2011* (Report, Australian Transaction Reports and Analysis Centre December 2013) 54.

42 Australian Transaction Reports and Analysis Centre, *Australian Government, Terrorism Financing in Australia* (Report, Australian Transaction Reports and Analysis Centre, Australian Government, 2014).

institutions in relation to ATMs up until the time of the CBA case seems to have been the risk that merchants could stuff illicit cash into ATMs and customers would be the unwitting vehicles for laundering that cash. The real risk, however, turned out to be the opposite, namely criminal customers, not merchants, stuffing illicit cash into ATMs.

Returning to the FATF report on Australia, it indicates in the opening pages that:

> Sector representatives whom the assessors interviewed did not report particular difficulties in applying AML/CFT measures for new technologies. Before introducing a new designated service, delivery method or technology, larger reporting entities would typically conduct a product risk assessment that included ML/TF risk, and determine the controls needed to mitigate these risks.[43]

This comment does not contain any specific references to financial institutions, or fuller content, to understand exactly what or whom is referred to when it is indicated that 'typically' larger reporting entities 'would conduct' product risk assessments before introducing the new technology. The reader is left wondering whether this might refer to all banks or only a few; to larger life insurance companies; or to any other financial institutions, such as securities dealers. Moreover, the comment is not consistent with the analysis that the evaluation team did of Australia's compliance with Recommendation 15. The comment could be deleted from the report without any impact on the evaluation of Australia's compliance with the FATF standards.

The analysis of Recommendations 15 in the Australian evaluation report was the following:

> 15.1. Australia has identified and assessed in its 2011 NTA [National Threat Assessment] the ML risks associated with

---

43 FATF and APG (2015), above n 39, 89 [5.37].

'electronic payment systems and new payment methods' which cover ATMs, credit/debit cards and stored value cards, online payment systems, online remittance and digital currencies ... Reporting entities are required under section 81 of the AML/CTF Rules to adopt and maintain an AML/CTF programme whose objective, consistently with section 84(2), is to identify; mitigate and manage ML/TF risk. The AML/CTF Rules further specify under Parts 8.1 and 9.1 the factors to be considered for the identification of ML/TF risk, in particular the types of services provided and the methods by which services are delivered. The same provisions also state that the AML/CTF programme must enable reporting entities to assess the ML/TF risk posed by all new designated services prior to introducing them to the market; all new methods of designated service delivery prior to adopting them; and all new or developing technologies used for the provision of a designated service prior to adopting them.

15.2. As described above, reporting entities are required to assess new services, methods of delivery and technologies prior to their adoption or use. However, other than the general obligation to assess the ML/TF risk (section 80 et seq. of the AML/CTF Act and Paragraphs 8.1.5 and 9.1.5 of the AML/CTF Rules), there is no specific explicit requirement for reporting entities to take appropriate measures to manage and mitigate the identified risks in the area of new technologies.[44]

The report then concludes that Australia 'demonstrated it had assessed ML/TF risks associated with some new products and technologies'. The report goes further and states that 'reporting entities were required to identify, mitigate and manage their ML/TF risks, but there is no specific obligation for new technologies. Recommendation 15 was rated largely compliant'.[45]

---

44 Ibid 161.

45 Ibid 162. The rating of *largely compliant* means, 'There are only minor shortcom-

Note that the analysis and conclusion in the FATF report does not indicate that financial institutions, including banks, had *actually assessed* the threat or risk associated with new technologies, including ATMs, nor does the analysis actually indicate that any type of process was utilised to assess that risk. Notwithstanding that, the overall rating assigned was a pass mark.

If the FATF report had actually drilled down into whether risk assessments had actually taken place by financial institutions, it is a possibility that the FATF assessors would have, or could have, detected a lack of such risk identification associated with IDMs and perhaps other forms of new technology used in the banking sector. According to the CBA, it did not, at the time, undertake a money laundering and terrorist financing risk assessment of its IDMs and implement mechanisms to manage the identified high ML/TF risks posed by IDMs. AUSTRAC had provided banks, including CBA, with a 'methodologies brief' identifying risk factors associated with those machines,[46] but no effective action was taken in response to it. And the FATF evaluation team did not reference that brief in its report.

In short, the CBA and the FATF evaluation team (in the author's view) had shortcomings. CBA did not conduct a required risk assessment of IDMs before their launch and the FATF did not ask whether they had done so (despite the clear wording of Recommendation 15), and consequently did not report the general failure of the banking sector (as opposed to the specific bank in question[47]) to do so in the 2015 report.

Would it have made a difference if the FATF evaluators had picked up on CBA's failure and reported more generally that there was a lack of

---

ings' with compliance in relation to any particular recommendation (see, FATF Assessment Methodology, above n 26, 13).

46 Chief Executive Officer of the Australian Transaction Reports and Analysis Centre and Commonwealth Bank of Australia, above n 29, 7 [33]–[34].

47 While FATF/APG reports do not, as a practice, specifically identify individual banks or other financial institutions by name in their reports, a significant failure to meet key obligations in the FATF Recommendations by large or dominant institutions in any given country can and does result in a notation in the report of a general failure to meet a specific requirements.

compliance with Recommendation 15? It is difficult to say. The FATF evaluators were only doing what the FATF policy-makers and body of previous reports on the subject had expected them to do, notwithstanding that the original intent of Recommendation 15, as reflected in its clear wording, requires a more thorough and stringent examination of the facts.

Whatever the outcome might have been, and whether the FATF evaluation team actually applied FATF Recommendation 15 properly, the CBA paid a high price for not doing what the plain wording of Recommendation 15 said and continues to say.

V. Conclusions

The FATF Recommendations contain important tools in the fight against money laundering and terrorist financing. But those tools are only as good as the degree to which they are properly implemented in a country and more widely within the international community. Otherwise, what might appear as small gaps in a country's, or a financial institution's, AML/CFT system may actually be 'gaping holes' (to quote from the epigraph) ripe for criminal exploitation.[48]

Enacting laws to give effect to the FATF Recommendations is more than a *recommendation* (in the small 'r' sense of the word) as was discussed at the beginning of this chapter. It is mandatory for countries who are members of the global anti-money laundering network consisting of the FATF and a number of regional bodies, such as the Asia/Pacific Group on Money Laundering, to create laws to combat criminals and terrorists and, in doing so, protect the integrity of the global financial system. But those obligations go beyond simply legislating. The obligations include requirements to undertake actions, even if there are no laws, including assessing the financial crime risks of new products and services. If those risk assessments are not in place, together with programmes to address the highest risks identified, then the 'gaping holes' turn into huge opportunities from criminal exploitation.

---

48 McKenzie, Baker and Mitchell, above n 1.

Contributors

David Chaikin

Dr David Chaikin is the Chair of the Discipline of Business Law and an Associate Professor at the University of Sydney Business School. David teaches and researches in Banking and Finance Law, International Financial Crime and the Law of Asset Protection. David has been a practising lawyer for more than 30 years and previously held the positions of Senior Assistant Secretary in the Australian Attorney-General's Department and Senior Legal Officer of the London-based diplomatic body, the Commonwealth Secretariat. He has been an expert advisor to the Financial Action Task Force, the Financial Services Council and the Australian Treasury's Panel on Whistleblower Protections. David has authored or edited books on corporate & trust structures, digital disruption, financial services regulation, corruption and money laundering. He has a Phd in Law from Cambridge University, a Master of Laws from Yale Law School and double degrees in law and commerce (accounting, finance and systems) from the University of New South Wales

Derwent Coshott

Dr Derwent Coshott is an Associate Lecturer at the Sydney Law School and regularly teaches at the University of Sydney Business School. His research focuses on the intersection of equity, property and contract law in the development and use of trust structures throughout the world, and has been published in leading international journals, such as the *Law Quarterly Review*. Derwent is also the co-author of the 6th edition of *Sale of Land in NSW: Commentary and Materials* and co-edited *Digital Disruption: Impact on Business Models, Regulation & Financial Crime*.

Matt Egerton-Warburton

Matt Egerton-Warburton is a Special Counsel in the Mergers & Acquisitions group in Sydney at King & Wood Mallesons, where he practices in mergers and acquisitions, joint ventures, equity capital markets and general corporate advisory work. Matt advises on international acquisitions, disposals and joint ventures across a wide range of industry sectors, including financial services, technology, insurance, energy and resources, agribusiness, media and telecommunications. His clients have included international corporates, sovereign wealth funds, state owned enterprises, investment and retail banks, hedge funds, private equity funds, venture capital funds and family offices. Matt has also represented issuers and underwriters in securities offerings in various jurisdictions including Hong Kong, Singapore, Malaysia, Philippines, Taiwan, Argentina, Australia, Canada, UK and US. Matt has worked in London, New York, Hong Kong and Sydney, and is a member of the Australian Institute of Company Directors and the Hong Kong Venture Capital Association. Matt is currently admitted to practice in NSW, Hong Kong and New York. Matt previously worked in politics as a press and policy advisor and was an executive director and founder of an internet start-up.

Rod Henderson

Emerging from a professional career with KPMG spanning 30 years as an international M&A tax partner, Rod founded his own startup, AcuTax, Australia's first automated online tax advisory app, based at the Tank Stream Labs innovation hub in Sydney. In addition, Rod continues to provide tax advice to growing Chinese companies and businesses, as well as helping businesses to solve complex tax problems. Rod has worked with the University of Sydney Business School, bringing his extensive professional experience, and ideas around tax and legal acumen, to contribute to the development of a new practical capstone course for students majoring in business law. In his spare time, as a singer songwriter, Rod is recording an album of his own songs under the working title Triple Denim.

Gordon Hook

Dr Gordon Hook is the Executive Secretary of the Asia/Pacific Group on Money Laundering (APG), a multi-lateral organisation of 41 countries and jurisdictions in the Asia-Pacific region responsible for the implementation of the international standards against money laundering and terrorist financing. Prior to his current position he practiced law as a partner in a Canadian law firm in Winnipeg in the 1980s and 1990s. He then served in the Royal New Zealand Navy (RNZN) as a senior legal officer which included a five-month tour in the Persian Gulf from November 2002 to April 2003 as the naval task force legal advisor during US led Operation Enduring Freedom. After serving in the RNZN he joined the New Zealand Ministry of Justice as the Manager of Criminal and International Law where he led a team responsible for New Zealand's AML/CFT reform programme. Gordon Hook holds a BA and MA from the University of Manitoba in Canada, a LLB from Dalhousie University in Canada, and a PhD in Law from Victoria University of Wellington in New Zealand. He is a Barrister and Solicitor of the Manitoba Queen's Bench and of the High Court of New Zealand.

Rachel Launders

Rachel is general counsel and company secretary at Nine Entertainment Co. Holdings Limited, leading a team which manages the diverse array of legal issues which arise across a media business. Prior to joining Nine Entertainment in 2015, Rachel was a partner at Gilbert & Tobin for many years where she specialised in mergers and acquisitions, corporate governance and commercial transactions. Rachel is a non-executive director of Gateway Lifestyle Group, an ASX200 listed entity which provides affordable housing solutions for a 50+ aged market. She is also a director and company secretary of Giant Steps, a charity which runs schools for children and young adults with autism in Sydney and Melbourne.

Michael Levi

Dr Michael Levi (MA, Dip Crim, PhD, DSc (Econ)) has degrees from Oxford, Cambridge, Southampton and Cardiff, and has been Professor of Criminology at Cardiff University since 1991. He is an Associate Fellow of the Royal United Services Institute and a Senior Fellow at RAND Europe. He has been conducting international research on the control of white-collar and organised crime, corruption and money laundering/ financing of terrorism since 1972. Current and recent posts include Member, European Commission Group of Experts on Corruption; Member, Center for Global Development Working Party on Illicit Financial Flows; President, US National White-Collar Crime Research Consortium; Member, Illicit Trade and Organized Crime Council, World Economic Forum; Member, Committee on the Illicit Tobacco Market, US National Academy of Sciences; Member, EC Proceeds of Crime Confiscation Expert Working Group and Asset Recovery Office Working Group; independent member, UK Statistics Authority Crime Statistics Advisory Committee. He is an advisor to Europol on its organised and internet crime threat assessments. In 2013 he was given the Distinguished Scholar Award by the International Association for the Study of Organised Crime, and in 2014 he was awarded the Sellin-Glueck prize for international and comparative criminology by the American Society of Criminology.

Dominic Millgate

Dominic was appointed Company Secretary of Boral Limited in July 2013, having been Assistant Company Secretary since November 2010. He has previously been legal counsel and company secretary for listed entities in Australia and Singapore and has held legal positions in London and Sydney. He is a Fellow of the Institute of Chartered Secretaries, is admitted to practice as a solicitor in NSW, and holds a finance degree from the University of New England and a law degree from the University of Sydney.

Juliette Overland

Dr Juliette Overland (LLB (Hons I) (QUT), PhD (ANU)) is the Associate Dean (Student Life), Associate Dean (Indigenous Strategy & Services) and an Associate Professor in the Discipline of Business Law at the University of Sydney Business School. Her research and teaching expertise focus on corporate law, particularly the regulation of securities markets, insider trading, and corporate crime. Juliette is recognised as a leading authority on the regulation of insider trading and she has published widely in this area, including a monograph titled *Corporate Liability for Insider Trading*. Juliette's research has examined issues concerning corporate social responsibility, the role of deterrence in sentencing convicted corporate criminals, and the effectiveness of insider trading regulations. In addition to her experience as an academic, Juliette has extensive practical experience as a corporate lawyer, having worked in leading Australian law firms and as the Australian legal counsel for a global technology company.

Printed in Australia
Ingram Content Group Australia Pty Ltd
AUHW020122021224
403587AU00003B/39

9 781925 984248